On This Rock

A Church Planting Sampler

Compiled by
Rev. Don Allsman, Rev. Dr. Don Davis,
Lorna Rasmussen, and Rev. Dr. Hank Voss

TUMI Press
3701 East Thirteenth Street North
Wichita, Kansas 67208

On This Rock: A Church Planting Sampler

The Urban Ministry Institute
3701 East 13th Street North
Wichita, KS 67208

ISBN: 978-1-62932-307-7

Published by TUMI Press
A division of World Impact, Inc.

The Urban Ministry Institute is a ministry of World Impact, Inc.

Table of Contents

Introduction. 7

Church Planting Overview 11

World Impact's Strategy for Church Planting 13

Preface: How to Use This Guidebook 17

Seeing the Big Picture (graphic) 29

Session 1: Seeing the Big Picture – Themes and Objectives . . . 30

What Is a Church? 32

Church Planting Overview 35

Session 2: Prepare – Themes and Objectives 44

Overview of Exercise Phases for
World Impact's Evangel School of Urban Church Planting . . . 46

Cross-Cultural Church Planting Principles 48

Theology of Culture and the Poor. 49

On World Impact's "Empowering the Urban Poor" 51

Our Distinctive: Advancing the Kingdom among the Urban Poor . . 57

Interaction of Class, Culture, and Race 65

Targeting Unreached Groups in Churched Neighborhoods . . . 66

The SIAFU Network – Assembling God's Warriors:
Toward a Strategy to Win the City. 67

The Great Tradition and Creedal Theology 73

The Story of God: Our Sacred Roots 75

There Is a River: Identifying the Streams of a Revitalized Authentic Christian Community in the City 76

Substitute Centers to a Christ-Centered Vision: Goods and Effects Which Our Culture Substitutes as the Ultimate Concern 77

The Picture and the Drama: Image and Story in the Recovery of Biblical Myth 78

From Before to Beyond Time: The Plan of God and Human History 79

The Theology of Christus Victor: A Christ-Centered Biblical Motif for Integrating and Renewing the Urban Church 80

Christus Victor: An Integrated Vision for the Christian Life and Witness 81

Church Planting Models and Strategies 83

Using Wisdom in Ministry: The PWR Process 85

Davis's Project Gauntlet: The Dirty Dozen Criteria for New Initiatives 95

Researching Your Community 97

Church Planting Models 110

Membership Commissioning Service: Anyname Fellowship Church 113

Church Planting Movements 115

Introduction: Sacred Roots, Church Planting, and the Great Tradition . . . 117

The Nature of Dynamic Church Planting Movements: Defining the Elements of Effective Church Planting Movements . 123

Creating Coherent Urban Church Planting Movements: Discerning the Elements of Authentic Urban Christian Community . . . 124

The Threefold Cord of Urban Cross-Cultural Church Planting Movements 125

A Model of an Urban Church Association 126

Church Planting Roles and Responsibilities 127

Responsibilities of a Church Plant Team Leader 129

Forming the Church Plant Team and Understanding the Roles . 130

Key Roles of a Church Planting Team 134

Responsibilities of a Coach (Multiple Team Leader) 135

Equipping the Church Plant Team Member:
Developing Workable Training Strategies. 136

Empowering Indegenous Leadership 137

Investment, Empowerment, and Assessment: How Leadership as Representation Provides Freedom to Innovate 139

Nurturing Authentic Christian Leadership 140

Summary of the Capstone Curriculum. 141

Fit to Represent: Multiplying Disciples of the Kingdom of God . 148

Discipling the Faithful:
Establishing Leaders for the Urban Church 149

Understanding Leadership as Representation:
The Six Stages of Formal Proxy. 150

Overview of TUMI's Resources on the Urban Poor 151

An Abridged Church Planting Bibliography 159

**Appendix:
World Impact's Church Planting Resources at a Glance . . 167**

Table of Contents:
Ripe for Harvest. 169

Table of Contents:
Planting Churches among the City's Poor, Volume 1 174

Table of Contents:
Planting Churches among the City's Poor, Volume 2 180

Prologue:
Planting Churches among the City's Poor, Volumes 1 and 2 . . 185

Table of Contents:
The Evangel Dean Handbook 192

Introduction

> We must be global Christians with a global vision because our God is a global God.
>
> ~ John Stott

It has been many centuries since the time our risen Lord commanded the amazed and primed apostles to go and make disciples of all people groups (Matt. 28.18-20). Endued with all power from the Father on high, our Lord commanded his disciples (and through them, the Church through the ages) to sacrifice their lives, gifts, and capacities to win a world that desperately needs to hear of the grace of our God. This command to go and make disciples, this simple yet revolutionary directive, gave birth to missions, and now today should shape everything that we are as believers, as congregations, as ministries and mission societies, and as movements under the authority of Christ. No higher call exists for the present generation of Christians than to do everything that we can to fulfill the commission of Christ to make disciples of the nations. This call is the critical call – for everyone who names his high name.

Our Lord Jesus affirmed the significance of his church in his recognition of Peter's confession of his messiahship in Matthew 16.15-18 (ESV):

> He said to them, "But who do you say that I am?" [16] Simon Peter replied, "You are the Christ, the Son of the living God." [17] And Jesus answered him, "Blessed are you, Simon Bar-Jonah! For flesh and blood has not revealed this to you, but my Father who is in heaven. [18] And I tell you, you are Peter, and on this rock I will build my church, and the gates of hell shall not prevail against it.

Jesus' unqualified conviction was that he would build his Church on the rock of Peter's confession, and that the very gates of hell would not be able to withstand its advance. The center of Christ's present-day work in the world is the calling out of his own from among the nations to become a part of his one, holy, catholic (universal), and apostolic Church. Wherever his Church exists in local assembly, so does that community also represent a living, vital outpost of the Kingdom of God in our time. Planting and sustaining healthy churches is elemental to the kingdom mission of Christ in this age.

This sampler represents a strategic smattering of the kind of resources contained in our recently published cadre of church planting materials. These are entitled *Ripe for Harvest*, our official textbook for the Evangel School of Urban Church Planting, *The Evangel Dean Handbook* to the

Evangel School, and our *Planting Churches among the City's Poor*, a two-volume reference compendium with the major resources we have used over the past twenty plus years of planting churches among the poor in the inner cities of America. Together, these books themselves include more than 1700 pages of material, so, in order to expose you to the breadth of the kinds of materials these volumes contain, we produced this sampler.

We organized this broad collection of articles and graphics under seven strategic categories from all four volumes:

- Church Planting Overview
- Theology of Culture and the Poor
- The Great Tradition and Creedal Theology
- Church Planting Models and Strategies
- Church Planting Movements
- Church Planting Roles and Responsibilities
- Empowering Indigenous Leadership

Under these themes you will find a plethora of sample miscellaneous materials from these four volumes: graphics, articles, essays, charts, exercises and an abridged church planting bibliography, all included to expose you to the wealth of resources contained in these four volumes on the perils and promise of church planting. Lastly, we have provided the Tables of Contents from the books themselves, i.e., *Ripe for Harvest*, *The Evangel Dean Handbook*, and the *Planting Churches among the City's Poor* two-volume reference works. (Please note: we have tagged each resource in the sampler so you can discern what resource a particular graphic or article is taken from).

This sampler represents the training materials of World Impact, a Christian missions organization which has ministered in the inner cities of America for more than forty years (*www.worldimpact.org*). We are deeply committed to facilitating church-planting movements by evangelizing, equipping and empowering the unchurched urban poor. World Impact's purpose is to honor and glorify God and to delight in him among the unchurched urban poor by knowing God and making him known. For us, the fastest, most efficient, and most powerful method to impact and transform urban poor communities is to plant healthy Christ-centered churches where the light and life of Jesus Christ is proclaimed and demonstrated for all to see. Our belief is that through the planting of healthy churches among the poor, the Holy Spirit will show his transformative power within and through the members of these neighborhoods.

Through the Spirit's leading, these churches will develop missional partnerships where kingdom-minded leaders and churches can collaborate together for mission and justice. We are trusting God to help us identify, equip, and empower a new generation of urban leaders who will through an empowered urban church demonstrate compassion and justice in the communities where they live and work. In our view, nothing is more critical or important for the sake of kingdom advance in the city than the planting of healthy assemblies of Christ, filled with disciples who are loving God with their whole hearts and their neighbors as themselves. These communities, indeed, are God's method of kingdom transformation in this lost world.

Our hope is that this sampler will trigger a desire for you to move from a mere taste of materials to the actual full texts which are available to you at our online store (www.tumistore.org). When our Lord rose from the dead, his revolutionary grace and conquering victory became accessible to the peoples of the world. The command to make disciples is directly linked to the missionary task of evangelism, equipping, and empowering urban folk through the work of church planting. This sampler provides a broad spectrum of our thinking and practice on urban cross-cultural church planting, including its theological, spiritual, missiological, and sociological components. Hopefully, a perusal of these diverse materials will provide you with a sense of our commitment to seeing the Great Commission fulfilled among the world's urban poor, and what we believe we will need to accomplish this.

Brother John Stott's quote at the beginning of this introduction says it well: "We must be global Christians with a global vision because our God is a global God." World Impact is striving to live up to its name, under the anointing and leading of the Holy Spirit. Our passion is to see the Kingdom of God declared and demonstrated in communities where Christ is neither known nor worshiped, in the poorest, most neglected neighborhoods in America and around the world. Our conviction is that planting churches and facilitating church plant movements is the fastest, most effective way to embrace a global vision of kingdom advance, starting here in the communities of the poor in the U.S. Our prayer is that this sampler may spark interest in you, our readers, to join us in this great campaign of winning the world's poor for Christ. The same Lord who confessed that he would build his Church on the Rock centuries ago is empowering his people today to plant churches and spawn new movements among the unreached around the world. Anyone who listens closely can still hear our Savior affirm his words that he declared to Peter so long ago: "On this rock I will build my church, and the gates of hell shall not prevail against it." Through his people, God's truth still marches on.

Rev. Dr. Don L. Davis
Director, The Urban Ministry Institute
Senior Vice President, Church and Leadership Development, World Impact
December 22, 2015

Church Planting Overview

Source:
Planting Churches among the City's Poor, Volume 1, pp. 288-291

World Impact's Strategy for Church Planting

Rev. Efrem Smith

"Crowns of Beauty: the indigenous and urban church planting initiative of World Impact."

Church Planting Purpose

Striving to plant as many churches as possible among the various cultures represented by the urban poor, in all of our cities and beyond.

1. **Credibility**
   - We are not a Para Church or Suburban Church coming into the city. We are an urban missions' organization with 40 plus years of incarnational, cross-cultural ministry experience.
   - Multiple staff that has over 20 years of Church Planting experience.
   - President and CEO, has extensive church planting, church planting training, and church planting design experience.
   - Significant research has been done on urban church planting through TUMI
   - We are unashamedly evangelical (Gospel, Christ, and Word-centered)
   - We are an interdenominational organization.

2. **Theology and Biblical Foundations**
   - Use Isaiah and Ezekiel to lift up significance of "Crowns of Beauty."
   - Embracing the Entire Epic of the Bible- "People of the Story"
   - Embracing the multi-ethnic, multicultural, urban, and liberating dynamic of the Bible.
   - Engaging the Kingdom of God and Christus Victor.
   - We are informed by the Great Tradition.
   - Planting urban churches which function as communities of theology, worship, discipleship, and witness.

Source: *Planting Churches among the City's Poor, Volume 1,* pp. 288-291

3. **The Movement's Missional Design**
   - The overall church planting movement will be one which reflects a, "Three-self" Missional Design (self-sustaining, self-reproducing, and self-governing).
   - We both plant churches with World Impact staff that transition to indigenous leadership and churches which begin with indigenous leadership.
   - ***The dynamics of our church planting movements will be known by shared spirituality, the ability to contextualize, and to create and sustain standardized practices and structures.***

4. **Values**
   - "The best way to restore Christians to vibrant theology, worship, discipleship, and outreach is to recapture the Church's identity as a People of the Story, through a re-connection to the Church's Sacred Roots." (Pg. 151- *Jesus Cropped from the Picture* by Allsman)
   - ***Connecting the Great Tradition, The Urban Poor, and Urban Church Planting***
   - We plant church associations, facilitate movements, and engage collaborative partnerships.

5. **Principles**
   - P.L.A.N.T. Acrostic
   - Indigenous Urban Leader Commitment
   - Historic Commitment to the Urban Poor and to Cities
   - A Missional (incarnational) Approach
   - Honoring multi-ethnic, multicultural, ethnic specific, and first generation-immigrant focuses
   - Planting churches with the existing urban church

6. **Supplemental Initiatives**
   - Urban Church Associations (UCA's)
   - World Impact Associates (WIA's)
   - The Urban Ministry Institute (TUMI)
   - SIAFU (Chapters and Leadership Homes)

Source: *Planting Churches among the City's Poor, Volume 1*, pp. 288-291

7. Three Expressions (all include assessing, training, chartering, and resourcing)

- HouseChurch (20-50 people)

  Can be understood as a small store in a shopping mall. Needs the connections to other small churches to both survive and thrive. Can meet virtually anywhere and can operate with a small footprint with little to no financial burdens. Can focus on a specific block, housing development, or network of families. A strong discipleship focus of indigenous leadership development can take place in this smaller connected group.

- Community Church (60-150 people)

  Can be understood as a grocery or convenience store. Focuses on a particular geographic identity and proximity, highlighting both the affinity, connection, and unique context of the congregation and the surrounding community. Developed around a deep calling and connection to a particular neighborhood. Will need a semi-stable place to meet (park, community center, or school). Partnership with other community churches is important.

- Mother Church (200+ people)

  Can be understood as a Walmart Superstore or Super Target. A missionally directed congregation that leverages its capabilities and gifts to be a . . .

  - Center of compassion, mercy, and justice ministries,
  - Nurturing headquarters for planting new churches, and
  - Incubator of other effective ministries among the unreached urban poor.
  - Note that a more rooted facility would be needed within this expression.

8. Church Planting Framework

- Church Planting School (Events, Training, Resources)
- A unified assessment, training, resourcing, and standardization strategy.
- Training World Impact Staff as coaches, mentors, and co-pastors.
- Assessing call and gifts of World Impact Staff/Indigenous Leaders. (school, assessment, charter)
- Partnerships (local churches, denominations and organizations)

Source: *Planting Churches among the City's Poor, Volume 1,* pp. 288-291

9. Delivery and Support

- Charter Budget-$15,000-$75,000 per church over 3 years and based on location/expression
- History and Current State- 72 churches planted and 45 active
- Goal: Plant 300 churches over the next 7 years (Cost: $15 million, Initial injection of $1 million)
- Target both C-1 and C-2 leaders.
- ***Church Resources Division will provide general oversight and Regions will implement.***
- ***Staff Needs – Begin with National Director, reporting to Don Davis and providing resourcing support to RVP's and EDM's.***
- Fund development strategy – National Planting Fund – split between regions with administrative percent, Regional Partnering Churches, and Regional Operating Budgets
- Factor in costs of Coaching, Church Plant in a Box ($100), Training, etc.
- Include Member Care as needed.
- Coaching and Mentoring Tools (Prepare, Work, and Review)
- Potential Goal Management Tool (Goal Span-Jeff Hunt)
- ***Set Chartering Goals in the areas of Theology, Worship, Discipleship, and Witness.***

Source:
Ripe for Harvest,
pp. 11-22

Preface
How to Use This Guidebook

The Evangel School of Urban Church Planting:
Boot Camp for Urban Church Planters

For more than forty years, World Impact has been dedicated to honoring and glorifying God and delighting in him among the unchurched urban poor by knowing him and making him known. An inner-city missions organization, our vision is to recruit, empower, and release urban leaders who will plant churches and launch indigenous church planting movements. We are convinced that God almighty desires to empower the urban poor to advance God's Kingdom in every city in America and beyond through the local church. Indeed, we believe that the Church's proclamation and demonstration of the Gospel is at the heart of God's kingdom mission.

Our *Evangel School of Urban Church Planting* trains and equips coaches, church planters, and church plant teams to plant healthy churches among the city's poor. In order to thrive in their efforts, urban church planters must adopt a clear theological vision and choose sound, culturally sensitive models and expressions of the church. They must apply biblical wisdom in order to effectively evangelize, equip, and empower unreached city folk to respond to the love of Christ, and take their place in representing Christ's Kingdom where they live and work.

This guidebook, the official text of the *Evangel School*, outlines a process of church planting that respects the unique cultures, environments, communities, and situations reflected in urban America. The PLANT approach outlined here provides practically wise and spiritually vital instruction to ensure that urban church planting teams will neither fail nor blunder as they seek to engage needy yet spiritually ripe unreached neighborhoods. The guidebook will guide teams through that process, with a focus on prayer, reflection, and wisdom to find God's unique call on each planter and team.

Filled with devotionals, seminars, exercises, and worksheets, with dozens of graphics, diagrams, and articles, this rich resource will empower church planting teams to design a strategy that will prove empowering to them. It can enable them to draft a course that is consistent with the vision God has given them to plant a healthy, Kingdom-declaring church, and launch movements that display the justice of the Kingdom among the oppressed. We are excited about both the interest and activity of many churches and denominations to establish outposts of the Kingdom

Source: *Ripe for Harvest,* pp. 11-22

in the neediest communities in our nation. Our prayer is that this resource contributes to that vision.

Church Planting – a Work of the Holy Spirit

Church planting is a spiritual activity. It is not like building a house or starting a business. It requires prayer, worship, fasting, teaching, discipline, and wisdom. Without the leading and provision of the Holy Spirit, we cannot possibly see a church planted among an unreached people group needing to know of the love of Christ. Knowing this, the objective of this book is to guide you in the process of discerning God's guidance in planting a church in another culture, in order to fulfill his call in the Great Commission. Our prayer is that by the time you complete the exercises in this book you will come to understand the truths of Gospel ministry in such a way that you will be *spiritually and tactically ready* to plant a church. As a result, each session opens with worship and a devotional and ends in an extended prayer time, which are both essential aspects of your preparation to plant a church.

The five sessions represent the span of a church plant team's effort and ministry in a neighborhood or among a people group, from your initial prayer gathering to the time of transitioning the new church with its pastoral leaders. Each session is specifically designed to help you develop a portion of your church-planting strategic plan. The final session will help you wrap up the details in order to have a plan that you can execute under the guidance of the Holy Spirit.

The Guidebook's Structure: Understanding the Session Format

This book assumes that the teams that the Lord calls will possess different visions for the church, and will approach their church planting in various ways. Whether you are planting a church in your own culture, or planting a church cross-culturally, you will need to chart your own unique journey, being informed by the principles presented in this book. Whether planting a church in your own culture (i.e., intra cultural mission), or facing the complexities related to cross-cultural mission, we have provided additional notes and/or questions that will prompt you to consider issues relevant to your unique church plant opportunity. We will identify these notes and insights in their own section entitled "Charting Your Own Course." These sections are written to prompt you to consider how the material relates to your particular vision and work. Spend good time reflecting on the issues and questions covered in this section in order to get maximum benefit from the material in each session.

Source: *Ripe for Harvest,* pp. 11-22

Each of the five sessions follows this pattern:

- ***Worship and Devotional***: some devotionals are available online (*www.tumi.org/churchplanting*) or you can teach your own devotional.
- ***Session Themes and Objectives*** will provide you with a general framework for both understanding and benefitting from the elements in each session. This section includes a listing of the main concept and objectives of each session, along with a key Scripture, a principle of spiritual warfare, the key principle of church planting, and a selected quote that helps illumine the session and its goals.
- ***Seminar Teaching*** on the important ideas you will need to consider before discussing your plan of action. Some of these seminars will be available as audio or video recordings at *www.tumi.org*. Many of the seminars are supported by helpful Appendices that should be carefully reviewed as part of the planning process. Each seminar concludes with a list of questions for group discussion.
- ***Team Exercises*** include a list of guiding questions to help you translate your discussion into concrete goals and action steps. The exercises are designed to be done together as a church-plant team, not individually or in isolation. Questions apply to the whole team unless otherwise noted. If you have not yet formed a core team (at least 2 others but no more than 10), make sure you do so before you start Session Two (Session One may be helpful in defining your vision so you can recruit a core team to join you).

  There are eight team exercises in the book, and each exercise includes five parts:

  - Guidelines
  - Instructions
  - Discussion Questions, Reading Assignments, or Worksheets
  - Prayer
  - Team Presentation

Source: *Ripe for Harvest,* pp. 11-22

The eight exercises build progressively on each other and are arranged around the PLANT acronym (see the table "Overview of Exercise Phases for World Impact's Evangel School of Urban Church Planting" in sessions 2-5). The table below lists the eight exercises in the order they appear.

Session	Team Exercise
Session 1, Team Exercise #1	Seeing the Big Picture: Establishing the Context
Session 1, Team Exercise #2	Seeing the Big Picture: Defining Values/Vision
Session 2, Team Exercise #3	Prepare: Be the Church
Session 3, Team Exercise #4	Launch: Expand the Church
Session 3, Team Exercise #5	Assemble: Establish the Church
Session 4, Team Exercise #6	Nurture: Mature the Church
Session 4, Team Exercise #7	Transition: Release the Church
Session 5, Team Exercise #8	Bringing It All Together: The Team Charter

- *Presentations*. One of the most helpful activities for your team will be sharing with other teams the results of your reflection and dialogue together. Each Session allows for you to share with others some of your more important insights, questions, and issues that you gleaned together from your Team Exercise discussion. Be open and observant during this activity – without a doubt, some of the best ideas you will hear will not necessarily be ones which you thought up! Allow the Lord to give you new ideas through the other team participants.
- *Charting Your Own Course*. Whether you are planting a church within your own culture, or within an association or denomination and you know what your make-up, governance, transition, and framework will be after the church is planted, this section is especially written for you. Here you will find specific notes of action steps or key principles that you should be aware of as you make plans to start the process of planting a church within your own culture or community. This section will ask you to bring

Source: *Ripe for Harvest*, pp. 11-22

your own, unique questions and context to bear on the material, for maximum benefit.

- ***Further Resources***: Here you will find additional tools and helpful resources (e.g., bibliographies, suggested materials) that can be of use to you over the life of your church plant.
- ***Appendices***: At the end of each session, you will see a listing of some key articles, graphics, and/or diagrams that are specifically related to the concepts in that lesson. All appendices can be found in the complimentary volumes connected with this guidebook entitled *Planting Churches among the City's Poor: An Anthology of Urban Church Planting Resources, Volumes I and II*. Please note: **These reference books are essential in order to receive maximum benefit from this guidebook. They should be purchased and used as a set.**

  This is why these books are offered with this guidebook in the TUMI store [*www.tumistore.org*] at a discount, although each book can also be purchased individually. Please ensure that you have copies of the anthology handy for the various seminars, exercises, and discussions that make up each session's work.

  The appendices are arranged at the end of each session, helping to both clarify and illumine the concepts and themes covered in the material. *Do not be alarmed if you see the same appendices referenced in different sessions*. This was done on purpose! If certain concepts need to be reiterated, underscored, or reemphasized, they may appear multiple times throughout the manual. Certain concepts are so fundamental that they will demand multiple looks, dialogues, and considerations. Do your best to think through the materials for the sake of bringing the key lessons of each session into greater focus, i.e., those tough concepts that you and your teammates will need to master along your church planting journey.

Coaching and Training with *Ripe for Harvest*

This book is designed to be best used in conjunction with the *Evangel Church Plant School*. Several issues should be highlighted as your regarding the materials both in *Ripe for Harvest* and its complimentary text, *Planting Churches among the City's Poor*.

The first issue is about **designations and terms**. Since *Planting Churches among the City's Poor* is essentially an anthology, we sought to preserve our earlier documents in their original form, and did not go back through the documents and revise the language used in our earliest schools. This is not a major difficulty, however, because although we use different

Source:
Ripe for Harvest,
pp. 11-22

terms than our earlier schools, we have maintained the same functions for the positions. Two terms need to be defined:

- In previous materials, the term used for the church planting supervisor or mentor to whom the team leader reported or received input from was called a ***Multiple Team Leader*** or ***MTL***. Now, in this volume and in our schools, we refer to this role as ***Coach***. All references to ***MTL*** or ***Multiple Team Leader*** in this volume or in *Planting Churches among the City's Poor* should be understand now as ***Coach***.
- Also, in past schools we used the term ***Team Leader*** for the person in charge of the church plant team and church plant effort. Now, we refer to the person fulfilling this role as the ***Church Planter***.

In terms of language, then, please remember that when you engage materials in the *Anthology* that cite *MTL* or *Multiple Team Leader*, they now ought to be understood as equivalent terms to *Coach*, and, the designation *Team Leader* is equivalent now to the designation *Church Planter*.

The second issue relates to ***the various uses and applications*** of *Ripe for Harvest* in the context of training and coaching church planters. *Evangel Schools* are offered around the world in conjunction with denominations, organizations, churches, and/or satellites of The Urban Ministry Institute (TUMI). For a list of currently scheduled schools, please go to *www.tumi.org/churchplanting*. Coaches, mentors, and planters can use *Ripe for Harvest* for church plant training in several ways.

To begin with, the normal mode of this guidebook's use will be a planter and his/her team attending a locally sponsored Evangel School training session. The exercises are designed for planters and their teams to reflect on the devotionals, seminar teaching, and then answer the questions in open dialogue. This is done to give them opportunity to clarify their own unique strategies and approaches as they plan out their engagement in a community or a people group, to plant a church.

Besides attending an *Evangel School*, a group of new church planters may decide to work through this book under the guidance of a church plant coach. Those using *Ripe for Harvest* in this way would be an example of a "Church Plant Cohort." The cohort may be sponsored by a denomination, a church planting group, or an Urban Church Association (UCA).

Source: *Ripe for Harvest*, pp. 11-22

A third way the book might be used is in a "one-on-one" context. A church planter and a church plant coach may decide to work through this book together doing the exercises in a one-on-one format. The one-on-one format still assumes that the church planter has a core team that participates in the process, but it allows the church planter and church plant coach to work through the team exercises and the PLANT process on a timeline that works best for their individual team.

Ultimately, it is the church planter who is responsible for leading the church plant team through the guidebook exercises. Yet our work with hundreds of urban church plants has convinced us that every Timothy needs a Paul. We encourage you to invite a trusted person to serve as a *Coach* throughout your planning process. A Coach can provide you with ongoing encouragement and challenge, giving you objective advice, assisting you when you get stuck, and holding you answerable for your target dates, as God leads.

Even if using this book in the one-on-one format, we suggest that you as a church planter and/or church plant team prepare presentations periodically for your coach to review and comment upon. You naturally could prepare such an overview presentation for each stage of your church planting, providing a clear snapshot of your planning for the upcoming phase. Presentations are a good way to ensure you are making your plans concrete enough to be executed.

Listed below is a representative sample of the kinds of questions that a Coach might consider in his/her coaching activities and process with a church planter and his/her team:

- How are the team members doing in their relationship with God? Are they regularly practicing their core spiritual disciplines?
- How are the team members' relationships with each other?
- How is their communication? Do they listen to each other? Is everyone being heard?
- Is there sufficient consensus within the team?
- Are they able to resolve issues as they come up?
- Do they understand the PWR (prepare/work/review) process? Are they showing indication that they will be able to flex and adjust their plan at a later time?
- Have they considered all the relevant points?
- Will they be able to implement their plans?

Source: *Ripe for Harvest*, pp. 11-22

- Are they teachable and open to the Lord, to the leader, and to one another?
- Did they understand the exercises and complete them satisfactorily?
- Is there strong leadership?
- Is the team and its members weighing their decisions in light of the Holy Spirit's leading and the principles of Scripture?

Obtaining Our "Church Planter's Tool Kit"

In addition to the guidebook and the anthology texts, we have put together a resource "kit" for church planters and their teams that provides a broad range of essential tools every church planter or team should possess as they prepare and begin their work to plant a church in the community God has called them to. If at all possible, obtain the tool-kit and familiarize yourself with these materials *before* you engage in the sessions included in this guidebook.

(Note: In the TUMI Store [*www.tumistore.org*], we have priced this kit affordably [the kit contains one each of the following] so you can obtain them all together, at a discount!)

- *Ripe for Harvest*. The fundamental resource guidebook for the Evangel School of Urban Church Planting
- *Planting Churches among the City's Poor: An Anthology of Urban Church Planting Resources, Volumes I and II*. A thorough and essential listing of World Impact's historical papers, diagrams, and insights into the issues and opportunities associated with urban cross-cultural church planting among the urban poor.
- *Jesus Cropped from the Picture: Why Christians Get Bored and How to Restore them to Vibrant Faith*. An insightful analysis of the reasons behind the demise of the American evangelical church, and how to fix it.
- *Sacred Roots: A Primer on Retrieving the Great Tradition*. A sequel to *Jesus Cropped from the Picture*, this is an informative introduction to the power of shared spirituality of the ancient church, and how a return to those roots can transform the contemporary church.
- *Fight the Good Fight of Faith*. A clear, concise, and biblical introduction to the first truths of the Christian faith (and TUMI's official pre-Capstone curriculum). It is designed especially for new Christians and helps them understand what the Bible says

Source: *Ripe for Harvest*, pp. 11-22

about participating in God's grand story through nine integrated lessons from the book of Ephesians.

- *The Heroic Venture: A Parable of Project Leadership*. A manual on how to plan, implement, and lead important ministry projects, using lessons gleaned from the Lewis and Clark expedition to help us chart the way.
- *Managing Projects for Ministry*. A TUMI Course textbook, this practical how-to manual lays out the specific activities in designing, implementing, controlling, and wrapping up effective ministry projects – done on time, within budget, and according to specifications.
- *TUMI Sacred Roots Annual*. A yearly thematic devotional guide that employs the Christian year and an annual theme to aid disciples to walk in shared spirituality as a body together.
- *The Church Year Calendar*. A tool based on the Christian year to help believers walk together throughout the year focused on the life and ministry of Christ.
- *The SIAFU Network Guidebook*: A one-step guidebook on how to mobilize men and women in the local church for mission to their community and ministry to one another.
- *The SIAFU Network Chapter Meeting Guide*: A practical guide to show you how to set up and conduct your SIAFU Chapter gatherings so that your members will feel welcomed, refreshed, and encouraged as they worship, testify, and challenge each other in Christ.
- *Let God Arise!* The longer title of this book explains a bit more about its content: *Let God Arise: A Sober Call to Prevailing Prayer for a Dynamic Spiritual Awakening and the Aggressive Advancement of th Kingdom in America's Inner Cities*. This short booklet lays out a rationale for why every local urban church needs to be deeply committed to prayer.

In addition to the excellent resources in this kit, we also recommend the following tools that provide helpful insight in your outreach to the community, discipling the faithful, and empowering emerging leaders as God raises them up:

- *Making Joyful Noises: Mastering the Fundamentals of Music*. A primer on music theory and leading effective worship leading.
- *Vision for Mission: Nurturing an Apostolic Heart*. This eight-session study course describes the heart of a church planter viewed through the lens of the men who "turned the world

Source: *Ripe for Harvest*, pp. 11-22

upside down" It is part of TUMI's Foundations for Ministry Series and available through local TUMI satellites or online at *www.tumistore.org*.

- *Focus on Reproduction, Module 12, The Capstone Curriculum*. This eight-session study on urban church planting is module 12 of 16 in TUMI's *Capstone Curriculum*. The other three modules in the urban mission track of the *Capstone Curriculum* also provide vital resources for urban church planters (e.g. training on spiritual warfare, evangelism, mission to the poor, theology of the city, mercy ministries, etc.) and are available through local TUMI satellites or online at *www.tumistore.org*.
- *Winning the World: Facilitating Urban Church Planting Movements*. This eight-session study on Church Plant Movements is part of TUMI's *Foundations for Ministry Series*. It provides an important big picture overview of what the Holy Spirit is doing around the world through Church Plant Movements. It encourages church planters and church plant coaches to make a paradigm shift from focusing on single church plants to movements of church plants. This course is available through local TUMI satellites and at both www.tumistore.org and at *www.biblicaltraining.org*.
- *Church Matters: Retrieving the Great Tradition*. This eight-session study is part of TUMI's *Foundations for Ministry Series*. It provides an overview of the history of the Church and its Great Tradition which is essential context for any church partners unfamiliar with the Church's "Family History." This course is available through local TUMI satellites and at *www.tumistore.org*.
- *Marking Time: Forming Spirituality through the Christian Year*. This eight-session study is part of TUMI's *Foundations for Ministry Series*. It provides a strategy for discipleship and shared spirituality in the church using the Christian year. For church planters who have never considered their theology of time, this course is absolutely essential. It introduces a simple and reproducible system for discipleship, preaching, and spiritual formation gleaned from the example of the early church – a church primarily made up of the urban poor. This course is available through local TUMI satellites and at *www.tumistore.org*.
- *Multiplying Laborers for the Urban Harvest: Shifting the Paradigm for Servant Leadership Education*. Each church planter must figure out how to develop new leaders and The Urban Ministry Institute (TUMI) was founded in 1995 to help church planters with this task. Multiplying Laborers is a book that lays out a system for how each local church or network of local churches can provide excellent theological training for leaders in their

Source: *Ripe for Harvest,* pp. 11-22

own ministry context. In 2015, over two hundred urban churches and urban ministries have launched satellite campuses for training their leaders. This book is available at *www.tumistore.org*.

Supplies for the Journey: *www.tumi.org*

Among other things, The Urban Ministry Institute designs and produces resources for urban mission, specifically for the planting and multiplication of churches, and the empowerment of church movements, especially among the poor. For instance, in addition to the booklet, *Let God Arise!*, you will find on our site a plethora of resources to help you lay the groundwork of your church plant in prayer through the larger collection of *Let God Arise!* Prayer Resources. There are a constellation of resources available for evangelism, equipping, and empowering (see especially the *Master the Bible System*, and the *SIAFU* Resources).

Perhaps the most significant resource available to your new church plant is the sixteen module Capstone Curriculum. The sixteen modules provide seminary quality training for your church plant team members and emerging leaders. One church in the Los Angeles area has trained over one hundred leaders and planted twenty churches in five countries using the Capstone Curriculum as their primary leadership development tool. If your church plant is interested in launching your own training center you may want to consider launching a TUMI satellite at your church at some point in the PLANT process. In short, be sure to browse our site and become familiar with the many helpful resources for church planting and church life at *www.tumi.org/churchplanting*.

We have recorded the videos for each Session Seminar, which are available for either viewing or download at the following web page *www.tumi.org/churchplanting*. Our intent is to make these church planting materials available to the broadest possible audience, providing individuals, denominations, local churches, Urban Church Associations (UCAs), organizations, and missions groups with quality, clear materials that can equip a new generation of church planters who can raise up outposts in the most dangerous and least empowered communities in America and around the world. We assume your interest in this guide-book and anthology reveals your sharing this passion, this church planting DNA and vision.

A Vision for Our Time

Please know, our singular end is to find ways to outfit, encourage, and resource as many as we can with the kind of training and tools that make church planting among the poor a constant and effective ministry for years to come. We are ever open to your comments and suggestions,

Source: *Ripe for Harvest,* pp. 11-22

so please, do not hesitate to contact us – if you want to partner or link arms with us as we strive to raise up outposts of the Kingdom in the neediest communities on earth.

Immediately following his encounter with the Samaritan woman, she ran into the town and said to the people that she had found a man who had told her all that she had ever done. Surely, she said, this must be the Christ! Meanwhile, the disciples returned from their errand to get food, and urged him to eat. Jesus told them that his food was to do God's will and to finish his work. Then he replied, "Do you not say, 'There are yet four months, then comes the harvest'? Look, I tell you, lift up your eyes, and see that the fields are white [ripe] for harvest (John 4.35 ESV). The name for this guidebook is derived from this statement of our Lord. We have lifted up our eyes on the unreached urban poor, and know them to be fields fully mature, ripe for harvest. It is in the spirit of this readiness that we write this volume, penned for those see the ripened fields and are ready to plant healthy churches among the poor in the cities of the world.

Remember what our Lord said of the dying millions, a word that still fits the urban poor today:

> Matthew 9.35-38 (ESV) – And Jesus went throughout all the cities and villages, teaching in their synagogues and proclaiming the gospel of the kingdom and healing every disease and every affliction. When he saw the crowds, he had compassion for them, because they were harassed and helpless, like sheep without a shepherd. Then he said to his disciples, "The harvest is plentiful, but the laborers are few; therefore pray earnestly to the Lord of the harvest to send out laborers into his harvest."

May the Lord send out laborers into his harvest, among the urban poor peoples of this world, and may his Kingdom advance among them, to the glory of God. We are convinced that God will surprise us all as he works on their behalf, in places which have yet to experience his saving grace and love.

Rev. Don Allsman
Los Angeles, CA

Dr. Hank Voss
Los Angeles, CA

Dr. Don L. Davis
Wichita, KS

Source:
Ripe for Harvest,
p. 29

Session 1
Seeing the Big Picture

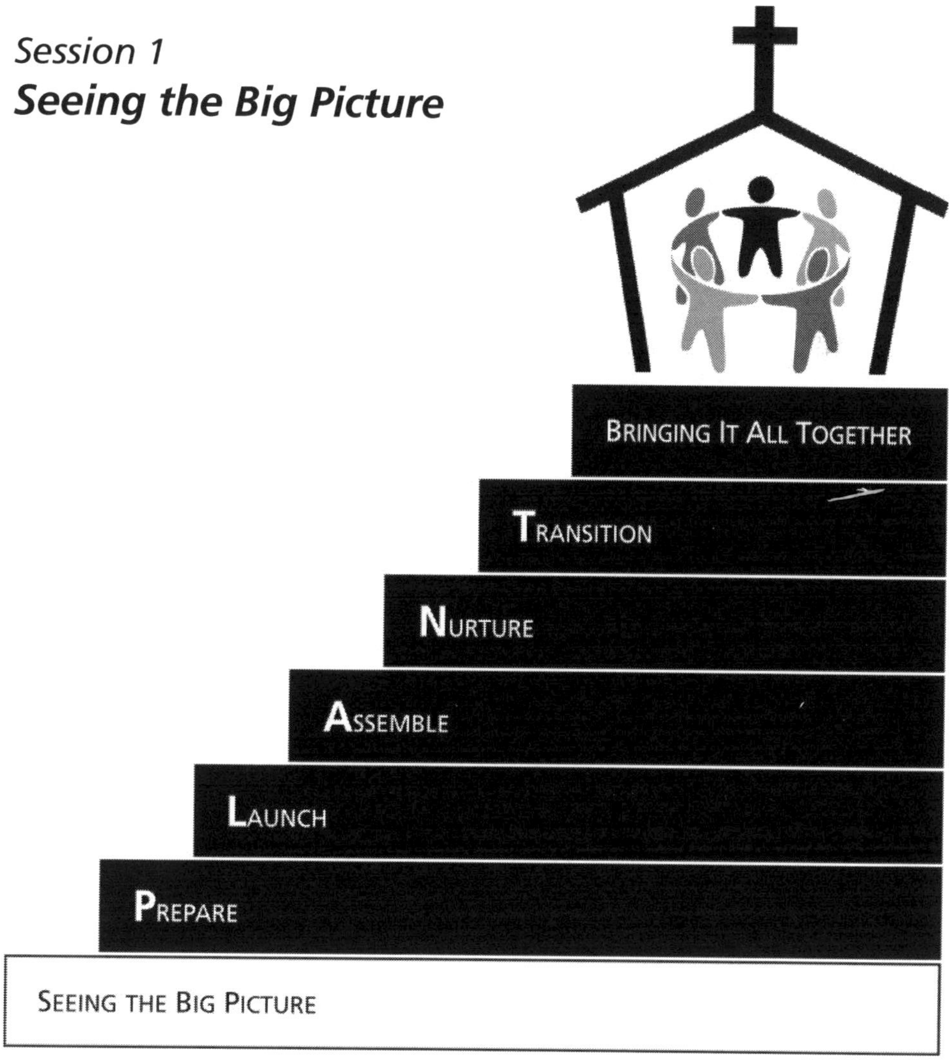

Bringing It All Together

Transition

Nurture

Assemble

Launch

Prepare

Seeing the Big Picture

Source:
Ripe for Harvest,
pp. 43-44

Session 1: Seeing the Big Picture
Themes and Objectives

Main Concept
Seeing the Big Picture

Objectives
After this session you will be able to:

- Articulate the critical theological and biblical themes which relate to God's purpose and plan for the church, and how the church advances God's Kingdom purpose throughout the world.
- Recite the three critical, historical expressions of the Church which define body life in the world today, and defend how those expressions help us better understanding how to plant churches among the urban poor.
- State the five basic phases of church planting, the PLANT acrostic, and express how those phases relate to the apostolic mission outlined in the New Testament.
- Define and share your values and vision regarding the call of God on you and your church plant team to plant a church in a particular community among a specific group of unreached people.
- Outline the rationale, steps, and results of the strategic PWR approach to planning and implementing God-given goals, and stewarding our resources for the sake of fulfilling our vision for mission and ministry.

Key Scripture
Eph. 6.10-18 (ESV) – Finally, be strong in the Lord and in the strength of his might. Put on the whole armor of God, that you may be able to stand against the schemes of the devil. For we do not wrestle against flesh and blood, but against the rulers, against the authorities, against the cosmic powers over this present darkness, against the spiritual forces of evil in the heavenly places. Therefore take up the whole armor of God, that you may be able to withstand in the evil day, and having done all, to stand firm. Stand therefore, having fastened on the belt of truth, and having put on the breastplate of righteousness, and, as shoes for your feet, having put on the readiness given by the gospel of peace. In all circumstances take up the shield of faith, with which you can

Context
Values/Vision
Prepare
Launch
Assemble
Nurture
Transition
Schedule/Charter

Source:
Ripe for Harvest,
pp. 43-44

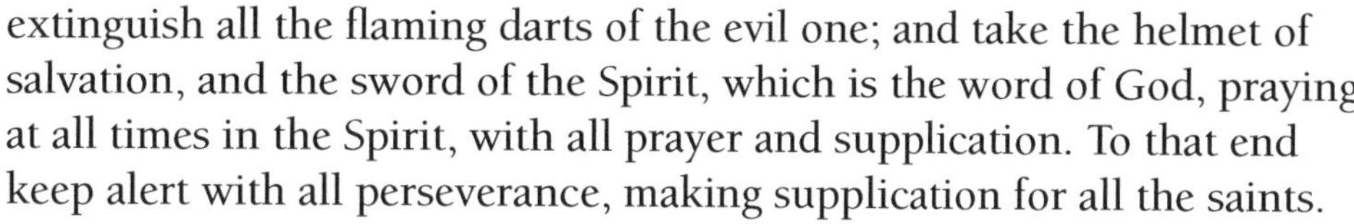
extinguish all the flaming darts of the evil one; and take the helmet of salvation, and the sword of the Spirit, which is the word of God, praying at all times in the Spirit, with all prayer and supplication. To that end keep alert with all perseverance, making supplication for all the saints.

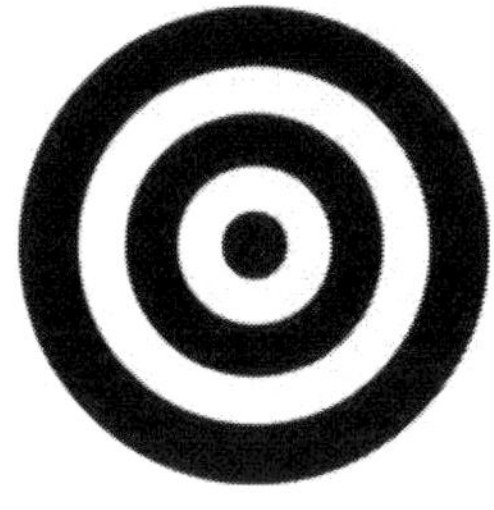

Principle of War: Objective
The clear aim of the activity; that which you are striving to accomplish

The Principle Related to Church Planting
In every activity, big and small, have a clear sense of your collective vision and your personal contribution to that vision.

> In preparing for battle I have always found that plans are useless, but planning is indispensable.
>
> ~ Dwight Eisenhower

Context
Values/Vision
Prepare
Launch
Assemble
Nurture
Transition
Schedule/Charter

Source: *Ripe for Harvest,* pp. 47-49

Seminar 1

What Is a Church?

Rev. Dr. Don Davis

The Church is the community of God's people who acknowledge Jesus as Lord, who carry out his purposes on earth, comprised of everyone past, present and future, from every place on the earth and throughout history. The Church is God's agent of the Kingdom of God, the body and bride of Christ, who as custodian of God's revelation has responded to his work in theology, worship, discipleship and witness (see *The Story of God: Our Sacred Roots*). Each local church is an embassy, serving as an outpost of his Kingdom.

There is a single story revealed in the Bible (see *Once Upon a Time*). The God of the universe, existing in three Persons (Father, Son, and Holy Spirit), is the Creator of all things, visible and invisible, who made human beings in His own image. Despite the rebellion of Satan and the first human pair, God sent a Savior who would overcome evil and win everything back for the glory of God.

In this unfolding drama, there is an objective foundation (the sovereign work of God in creation, Israel, and Christ) and a subjective response (the Church's participation in God's Kingdom). On the objective side, the Father is the Author and Director of the Story, the Son is the Champion and Lead Actor of the Story, and the Spirit is the Narrator and Interpreter of the Story. The Bible is the Script and Testimony of the Story.

On the subjective side, the People of the Story respond in orthodox theology as confessors of the faith, worship together as royal priests, are formed as disciples of Christ as sojourners in this world, and witness to God's love as his holy ambassadors. This understanding creates the foundation for every expression in a local church (see *Christus Victor: An Integrated Vision for the Christian Life and Witness*) including doctrine, use of gifts, spirituality, justice and compassion, evangelism and mission, and worship.

Context
Values/Vision
Prepare
Launch
Assemble
Nurture
Transition
Schedule/Charter

The Church is called to faithfully embody and defend God's revelation through the apostle's testimony, fulfilling its identity as one, holy, universal, and apostolic community (see *There Is a River*). The Church is to faithfully pass down what the Spirit gave to Christ's people in terms of what they believe, how they are to worship, and what their Scriptures would be. These foundational beliefs undergird the faith for all believers, everywhere, and is called the "Great Tradition" (see *The Nicene Creed*) which is embraced by all orthodox believers. This represents the

Source: *Ripe for Harvest,* pp. 47-49

teaching and practice of the apostles, written in the Bible, summarized in the creeds and councils of the Church, and defended by believers throughout history.

Church planting is simply an extension of the subjective expression of this Grand Cosmic Drama. A church plant is a new leaf on the Tree of God's design, going back to its Sacred Roots. Our identity is based on the guardianship and cross-cultural transference of the Great Tradition, which guards against heresy, sectarianism, syncretism, schism and pragmatism.

Once we see the broad landscape of the Church (big "C") we can then think more responsibly and clearly about the church (little "c"). In World Impact's conceptual dictionary, we acknowledge that the Church has historically and practically today expressed its community in three ways. These expressions will prove to be essential in our outworking of church planting among city folk, and encompasses all facets of our church planting strategy (including assessment for church planters, training and chartering church plant teams, and providing resources and directions through our coaches and funding).

(The purposes of these expressions is not to determine the absolute line between, say, 50 and 51 members in a church. Obviously, these numbers are not given for hard-and-fast distinctions between expressions. Rather, the numbers are meant to help provide us with a sense of the congregations regular, ongoing, size and makeup. Churches breathe in their membership, but do tend to settle at a particular attendance within margins. Do not see the numbers as absolute boundaries but rather as suggestive guidelines in terms of how a particular church tends to grow and function.)

Our three expressions are as follows:

The Small Church (or "house church," 20-50 or so people).
The small (or house) church can be understood as a *small store in a shopping mall*. It needs the connections to other small churches to both survive and thrive. Small churches are able to meet virtually anywhere and can operate with a tiny footprint with little to no financial burdens. They can focus on a specific block, housing development, or network of families. This expression allows for a strong discipleship focus of indigenous leadership development which can take place in this smaller connected group.

Community Church (60-150 or so people)
The community church is the most common expression of church, numerically speaking, in the world today. This expression can be

Context
Values/Vision
Prepare
Launch
Assemble
Nurture
Transition
Schedule/Charter

Source: *Ripe for Harvest,* pp. 47-49

understood as a *grocery or convenience store in a neighborhood or community*. This expression focuses on a particular geographic identity and proximity, highlighting the affinity, connection, and unique context of the congregation and the surrounding community. It is developed around a deep calling and connection to a particular neighborhood, and typically requires a semi-stable place to meet (e.g., a park, community center, or school). This expression especially depends on and is enriched by explicit partnerships formed with other community churches, which effectively strengthens and feeds their growth and mission as individual assemblies.

Mother Church (200+ people)
The mother church (or "hub church") represents a larger assembly of believers, and can be understood as *a Walmart Superstore or Super Target, a store which houses a number of select entities that supply its patrons with many choices and opportunities*. This kind of church, which has both the economic and spiritual resources for multiplication, can leverage its resources and capabilities to become both a sending/empowering church which reproduces itself many times over. Ideally, a mother or hub church is a congregation that is lead by clear missional intents that allow it to leverage its capabilities and gifts to become a center of compassion, mercy, and justice ministries. It can also come to serve as the nurturing headquarters for church planters and ministry starters, and can easily operate as an incubator of other effective ministries among the unreached urban poor. Such an expression usually is more rooted in a particular built-to-suit facility that allows it to leverage these kinds of capabilities.

Review the following appendices in *Planting Churches among the City's Poor: An Anthology of Urban Church Planting Resources* (please refer to the Appendix Table at the end of this session in order to find the location of each document listed below, i.e., its volume and page number), and then answer together the questions under Seminar Group Discussion.

- The Story of God: Our Sacred Roots
- Once Upon a Time: Understanding Our Church's Place in the Story of God
- *Christus Victor*: An Integrated Vision for the Christian Life and Witness
- The Theology of *Christus Victor*: A Christ-Centered Biblical Motif for Integrating and Renewing the Urban Church
- There Is a River: Identifying the Streams of a Revitalized Christian Community in the City
- The Nicene Creed

Context
Values/Vision
Prepare
Launch
Assemble
Nurture
Transition
Schedule/Charter

Source: *Ripe for Harvest,* pp. 51-59

Seminar 2

Church Planting Overview

Rev. Dr. Don L. Davis

How to PLANT a Church

I. Overview

A. Evangelize, equip, empower

B. PLANT

1. Prepare: Be the Church
2. Launch: Expand the Church
3. Assemble: Establish the Church
4. Nurture: Mature the Church
5. Transition: Release the Church

C. The steps

1. Evangelize: Prepare, Launch
2. Equip: Assemble, Nurture
3. Empower: Transition

Context
Values/Vision
Prepare
Launch
Assemble
Nurture
Transition
Schedule/Charter

Evangelize

Source:
Ripe for Harvest,
pp. 51-59

Mark 16.15-18 (ESV) – And he said to them, "Go into all the world and proclaim the gospel to the whole creation. [16] Whoever believes and is baptized will be saved, but whoever does not believe will be condemned. [17] And these signs will accompany those who believe: in my name they will cast out demons; they will speak in new tongues; [18] they will pick up serpents with their hands; and if they drink any deadly poison, it will not hurt them; they will lay their hands on the sick, and they will recover."

II. Prepare: Be the Church

Acts 16.25 (ESV) - About midnight Paul and Silas were praying and singing hymns to God, and the prisoners were listening to them.

A. Principle: A church is birthed from an existing church (we have to BE the church before we can plant the church).

1. We reproduce after our own kind. We do not start churches *ex nihilo*, but from other churches. We have an organic link from church to church back to Pentecost; to the Apostles; to Israel; to the Trinity. Community has been eternally existent; we are a part of that stream.

2. As in families, parents birth children, raise them in their homes and prepare them to be parents. Offspring bear our name and character. They share our biology and nurture. This intimacy is needed to create and sustain a church-planting movement. We do not distinguish the spirituality of training leaders from the spirituality of cross-cultural church planters.

3. New congregations will share our vision, doctrine, spiritual discipline, mission and finances. There is no distinction between the new congregation and the sent team.

4. The "P" of PLANT recognizes that the church exists as soon as the team is formed. Paul's team WAS the church in Philippi before Lydia's household joined them. Launch simply adds to the existing church.

Context
Values/Vision
Prepare
Launch
Assemble
Nurture
Transition
Schedule/Charter

Source:
Ripe for Harvest,
pp. 51-59

B. Elements of Prepare

1. Seek God's leading to select an unchurched target area or population (which may include demographic and ethnographic studies).

2. Form a church-plant team, the initial church which community believers can join.

3. Select a reproducible model to contextualize standard Church practices.

4. Initiate discussions about associations, denominations or other affiliations.

II. Launch: Expand the Church

Acts 2.47 (ESV) - And the Lord added to their number day by day those who were being saved.

A. Principle: Begin inviting people to join the community

B. Elements of Launch

1. Invite others (mature or new believers) to join the church.

2. Conduct evangelism to add to the existing church.

3. Follow up new converts

Context
Values/Vision
Prepare
Launch
Assemble
Nurture
Transition
Schedule/Charter

Equip

Source: *Ripe for Harvest,* pp. 51-59

Eph. 4.11-16 (ESV) – And he gave the apostles, the prophets, the evangelists, the pastors and teachers, [12] to equip the saints for the work of ministry, for building up the body of Christ, [13] until we all attain to the unity of the faith and of the knowledge of the Son of God, to mature manhood, to the measure of the stature of the fullness of Christ, [14] so that we may no longer be children, tossed to and fro by the waves and carried about by every wind of doctrine, by human cunning, by craftiness in deceitful schemes. [15] Rather, speaking the truth in love, we are to grow up in every way into him who is the head, into Christ, [16] from whom the whole body, joined and held together by every joint with which it is equipped, when each part is working properly, makes the body grow so that it builds itself up in love.

IV. Assemble: Establish the Church

Heb. 10.25 (ESV) - not neglecting to meet together, as is the habit of some, but encouraging one another, and all the more as you see the Day drawing near.

A. Principle: Bring the church to a place where it can be announced in the community as a functioning Body.

B. Elements of Assemble

1. Train others through cell groups or Bible studies to follow up and disciple new believers.

2. Continue evangelism with *oikos* groups.

3. Identify and train emerging leaders, focusing on preparing leaders for Transition at a satellite campus of The Urban Ministry Institute (TUMI).

4. Assemble the groups where the Word is rightly preached, the sacraments are rightly administered and discipline is rightly ordered.

Context
Values/Vision
Prepare
Launch
Assemble
Nurture
Transition
Schedule/Charter

Source:
Ripe for Harvest,
pp. 51-59

5. Announce to the neighborhood the beginning of public worship.

V. Nurture: Mature the Church

1 Pet. 4.10 (ESV) - As each has received a gift, use it to serve one another, as good stewards of God's varied grace.

A. Principle: Leaders observe and practice their developing skills in a church with real people, identities and structures, under leadership that ensures consistent practices.

1. Leaders must be developed in the context of community, using the same theological, strategic, and Church practices that ensure replication from one church to another. For example, when an emerging leader learns how to serve communion at the mother church, s/he knows how to lead communion at the daughter church plant.

2. The contextualization of the standard Church practices must be designed to make it easy to train leaders and export to new churches. Structures facilitate and enable innovation.

B. Elements of Nurture

1. Use the Church Year calendar to disciple the congregation.

2. Train others to serve and lead through individual and group discipleship.

3. Encourage believers to exercise their gifts in the church.

4. Assign responsibility to the faithful (deacons, elders, future pastors).

Context
Values/Vision
Prepare
Launch
Assemble
Nurture
Transition
Schedule/Charter

Empower

Source:
Ripe for Harvest,
pp. 51-59

> Acts 20.28 (ESV) – Pay careful attention to yourselves and to all the flock, in which the Holy Spirit has made you overseers, to care for the church of God, which he obtained with his own blood.
>
> Acts 20.32(ESV) – And now I commend you to God and to the word of his grace, which is able to build you up and to give you the inheritance among all those who are sanctified.

VI. Transition: Release the Church

2 Tim. 2.2 (ESV) - and what you have heard from me in the presence of many witnesses entrust to faithful men who will be able to teach others also.

A. Principle: Make ready the release of cross-cultural church planters to pass the baton to indigenous leadership.

B. Elements of Transition

1. Commission faithful indigenous leaders to be deacons, elders and pastors.
2. Commission the church to be part of a self-governing, self-supporting and self-reproducing movement.
3. Join a denomination or association for fellowship, support and joint-ministry activity.
4. Begin reproducing a new church plant.

Evanglize

PREPARE: Be the Church

- Seek God's leading to select an unchurched target area or population.
- Form a church-plant team, the initial church which community believers can join.

Source:
Ripe for Harvest,
pp. 51-59

- Select a reproducible model to contextualize standard Church practices.
- Initiate discussions about associations, denominations or other affiliations.

LAUNCH: Expand the Church

- Invite others (mature or new believers) to join the church.
- Conduct evangelism to add to the existing church.
- Follow up new converts using "Fight the Good Fight of Faith."

Equip

ASSEMBLE: Establish the Church

- Train others through cell groups or Bible studies to follow up and disciple new believers.
- Continue evangelism with *oikos* groups.
- Identify and train emerging leaders at a satellite campus of TUMI.
- Assemble the groups where the Word is rightly preached, the sacraments are rightly administered and discipline is rightly ordered.
- Announce to the neighborhood the beginning of public worship.

NURTURE: Mature the Church

- Use the Church Year calendar to disciple the congregation.
- Train others to serve and lead through individual and group discipleship.
- Encourage believers to exercise their gifts in the church.
- Assign responsibility to the faithful (deacons, elders, future pastors).

Empower

TRANSITION: Release the Church

- Commission faithful indigenous leaders to be deacons, elders and pastors.
- Commission the church to be part of a self-governing, self-supporting and self-reproducing movement.
- Join a denomination or association for fellowship, support and joint-ministry activity.
- Begin reproducing a new church plant.

Context
Values/Vision
Prepare
Launch
Assemble
Nurture
Transition
Schedule/Charter

Source: *Ripe for Harvest,* pp. 51-59

Pauline Precedents from Acts: The Pauline Cycle

1. Missionaries Commissioned: Acts 13.1-4; 15.39-40; Gal. 1.15-16.
2. Audience Contacted: Acts 13.14-16; 14.1; 16.13-15; 17.16-19.
3. Gospel Communicated: Acts 13.17-41; 16.31; Rom. 10.9-14; 2 Tim. 2.8.
4. Hearers Converted: Acts. 13.48; 16.14-15; 20.21; 26.20; 1 Thess. 1.9-10.
5. Believers Congregated: Acts 13.43; 19.9; Rom 16.4-5; 1 Cor. 14.26.
6. Faith Confirmed: Acts 14.21-22; 15.41; Rom 16.17; Col. 1.28; 2 Thess. 2.15; 1 Tim. 1.3.
7. Leadership Consecrated; Acts 14.23; 2 Tim. 2.2; Titus 1.5.
8. Believers Commended; Acts 14.23; 16.40; 21.32 (2 Tim. 4.9 and Titus 3.12 by implication).
9. Relationships Continued: Acts 15.36; 18.23; 1 Cor. 16.5; Eph. 6.21-22; Col. 4.7-8.
10. Sending Churches Convened: Acts 14.26-27; 15.1-4.

The "Pauline Cycle" terminology, stages, and diagram are taken from David J. Hesselgrave, *Planting Churches Cross-Culturally,* 2nd ed. Grand Rapids: Baker Book House, 2000.

"Evangelize, Equip, and Empower" and "P.L.A.N.T." schemas for church planting taken from *Crowns of Beauty: Planting Urban Churches Conference Binder* Los Angeles: World Impact Press, 1999.

Context
Values/Vision
Prepare
Launch
Assemble
Nurture
Transition
Schedule/Charter

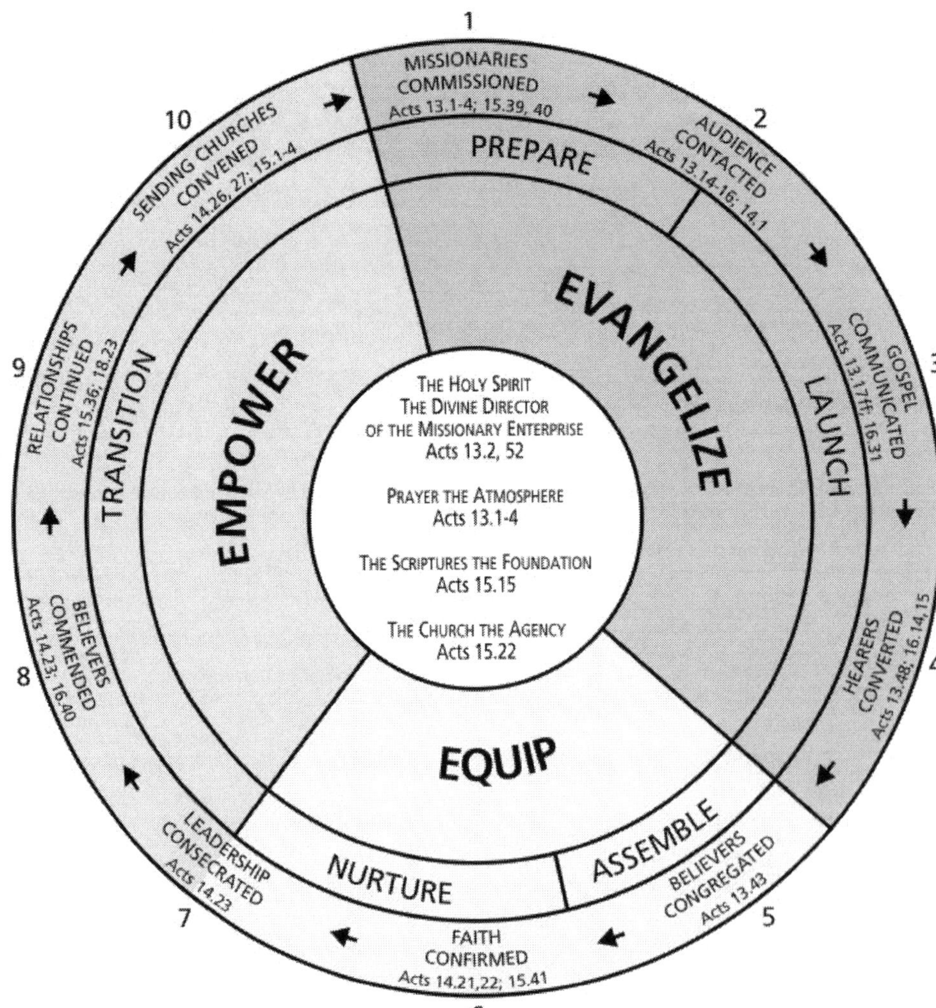

Source:
Ripe for Harvest,
p. 51-59

Ten Principles of Church Planting

1. **Jesus is Lord.** (Matt. 9.37-38) All church plant activity is made effective and fruitful under the watch care and power of the Lord Jesus, who himself is the Lord of the harvest.
2. **Evangelize, Equip, and Empower unreached people to reach people.** (1 Thess. 1.6-8) Our goal in reaching others for Christ is not only for solid conversion but also for dynamic multiplication; those who are reached must be trained to reach others as well.
3. **Be inclusive: whosoever will may come.** (Rom. 10.12) No strategy should forbid any person or group from entering into the Kingdom through Jesus Christ by faith.
4. **Be culturally neutral: Come just as you are.** (Col. 3.11) The Gospel places no demands on any seeker to change their culture as a prerequisite for coming to Jesus; they may come just as they are.
5. **Avoid a fortress mentality.** (Acts 1.8) The goal of missions is not to create an impregnable castle in the midst of an unsaved community, but a dynamic outpost of the Kingdom which launches a witness for Jesus within and unto the very borders of their world.
6. **Continue to evangelize to avoid stagnation.** (Rom. 1.16-17) Keep looking to the horizons with the vision of the Great Commission in mind; foster an environment of aggressive witness for Christ.
7. **Cross racial, class, gender, and language barriers.** (1 Cor. 9.19-22) Use your freedom in Christ to find new, credible ways to communicate the kingdom message to those farthest from the cultural spectrum of the traditional church.
8. **Respect the dominance of the receiving culture.** (Acts 15.23-29) Allow the Holy Spirit to incarnate the vision and the ethics of the Kingdom of God in the words, language, customs, styles, and experience of those who have embraced Jesus as their Lord.
9. **Avoid dependence.** (Eph. 4.11-16) Neither patronize nor be overly stingy towards the growing congregation; do not underestimate the power of the Spirit in the midst of even the smallest Christian community to accomplish God's work in their community.
10. **Think reproducibility.** (2 Tim. 2.2; Phil. 1.18) In every activity and project you initiate, think in terms of equipping others to do the same by maintaining an open mind regarding the means and ends of your missionary endeavors.

Context
Values/Vision
Prepare
Launch
Assemble
Nurture
Transition
Schedule/Charter

Source:
Ripe for Harvest,
pp. 131-132

Session 2: Prepare
Themes and Objectives

Main Concept
Prepare: Be the Church

Objectives
After this session you will be able to:

- Articulate the basic themes related to effective church planting preparation, including seeking God for his leading regarding the target population, the community, the formation of the team, the expressions of church you wish to plant, and your initial discussion of what association, denomination or affiliations you will make.
- Recite the importance of using our freedom in Christ to respect the receiving culture of those among whom we are planting a church.
- Despite the target population of our church plant, state the basic concepts which make up a biblical theology of the poor, which highlights God's call of and our corresponding respect for them, their election according to God's grace, and their call to lead in matters of the Kingdom of God.
- Define the basic characteristics of effective team play, and how your team can enhance its ability to function more effectively together in your efforts.
- Outline generally the standard practices you intend to incorporate into your church life (i.e., its theology, worship, spiritual formation, and witness) in the expression of church you will plant.

Key Scripture
Eph. 5.15-17 (ESV) – Look carefully then how you walk, not as unwise but as wise, [16] making the best use of the time, because the days are evil. Therefore do not be foolish, but understand what the will of the Lord is.

Context
Values/Vision
Prepare
Launch
Assemble
Nurture
Transition
Schedule/Charter

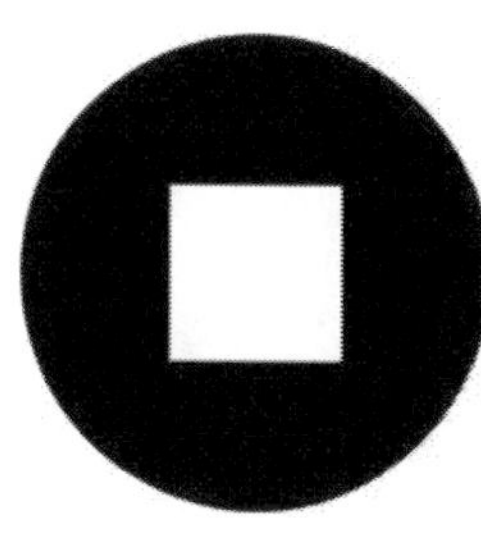

Source:
Ripe for Harvest,
pp. 131-132

Principle of War: Simplicity
Simple solutions and strategies are preferred over complex ones.

The Principle Related to Church Planting
Keep it simple; use only enough complexity to achieve victory.

> Warfare is a chaotic and unpredictable undertaking. Elaborate plans quickly come apart under the stress of combat. Large, elaborate and complex military organizations do require planning to keep them going and it's not easy to keep the procedures simple. The quality of your leaders and their ability to do the right thing in unison is the key.
>
> ~ James F. Dunnigan

Context
Values/Vision
Prepare
Launch
Assemble
Nurture
Transition
Schedule/Charter

Overview of Exercise Phases for World Impact's Evangel School of Urban Church Planting

World Impact

	Definition and Purpose	As Relates to Parent-Child Metaphor
Prepare	***Definition*** Forming a team of called members who ready themselves to plant a church under the Holy Spirit's guidance ***Purpose*** Seek God regarding the target population and community, the formation of your church plant team, organizing strategic intercession for the community, and doing research on its needs and opportunities	Decision and Conception
Launch	***Definition*** Penetrating the selected community by conducting evangelistic events among the target population ***Purpose*** Mobilize team and recruit volunteers to conduct ongoing evangelistic events and holistic outreach to win associates and neighbors to Christ	Pre-natal Care
Assemble	***Definition*** Gathering the cells of converts together to form a local assembly of believers, announcing the new church to the neighbors in the community ***Purpose*** Form cell groups, Bible studies, or home fellowships for follow-up, continued evangelism, and ongoing growth toward public birth of the church	Childbirth
Nurture	***Definition*** Nurturing member and leadership discipleship, enabling members to function in their spiritual gifts, and establishing solid infrastructure within the Christian assembly ***Purpose*** Develop individual and group discipleship by filling key roles in the body based on burden and gifting of members	Growth and Parenting
Transition	***Definition*** Empowering the church for independence by equipping leaders for autonomy, transferring authority, and creating structures for financial independence ***Purpose*** Commission members and elders, install pastor, and foster church associations	Maturity to Adulthood

Source: *Ripe for Harvest,* pp. 186-187

Question Focus During Dialogue	Cardinal Virtue and Critical Vices	Bottom Line
Questions about: • preparing your team • the target community • strategic prayer initiatives • demographic studies	***Virtue*** Openness to the Lord ***Vices*** Presumption and "paralysis of analysis"	Cultivate a period of listening and reflecting
Questions about: • character and number of evangelistic events • communication and advertisement of events • recruiting and coordinating volunteers • identity and name of the outreach	***Virtue*** Courage to engage the community ***Vices*** Intimidation and haughtiness	Initiate your engagement with boldness and confidence
Questions about: • follow-up and incorporation of new believers • make-up of small group life • the character of public worship • initial church structures and procedures • initial body life and growth • cultural friendliness of the church	***Virtue*** Wisdom to discern God's timing ***Vices*** Impatience and cowardice	Celebrate the announcement of your body with joy
Questions about: • discipling individuals and leaders • helping members identify gifts and burdens (teams) • credentials for leadership • church order, government, discipline	***Virtue*** Focus upon the faithful core ***Vices*** Neglect and micro-management	Concentrate on investing in the faithful
Questions about: • incorporation • affiliations and associations • transferring leadership • missionary transition • ongoing reproduction	***Virtue*** Dependence on the Spirit's ability ***Vices*** Paternalism and quick release	Pass the baton with confidence in the Spirit's continued working

Cross-Cultural Church Planting Principles

World Impact

1	Jesus is Lord.	Matthew 9.37-38
2	Evangelize, Equip, and Empower unreached people to reach people.	1 Thessalonians 1.6-8
3	Be inclusive: Whosoever will may come.	Romans 10.12
4	Be culturally neutral: Come just as you are.	Colossians 3.11
5	Avoid a fortress mentality.	Acts 1.8
6	Continue to evangelize to avoid stagnation.	Romans 1.16-17
7	Cross ethnic, class, gender, and language barriers.	1 Corinthians 9.19-22
8	Respect the dominance of the receiving culture.	Acts 15.23-29
9	Avoid dependence.	Ephesians 4.11-16
10	Think reproducibility.	2 Timothy 2.2; Philippians 1.18

Source: *Planting Churches among the City's Poor,* p. 254

Theology of Culture and the Poor

Source:
Ripe for Harvest,
pp. 195-200

On World Impact's "Empowering the Urban Poor"

Rev. Dr. Don L. Davis

Since our founding more than forty years ago, World Impact has spoken prophetically regarding God's election of the poor, the benign neglect of the evangelical church of America's inner city poor, and the need for evangelism, discipleship, and church planting in unreached urban poor communities. We believe that credible urban mission must demonstrate the Gospel, testifying in both the proclaimed word and concrete action. In light of this, we have emphasized living in the communities we serve, ministering to the needs of the whole person, as well as to the members of the whole urban family. We have sought this witness with a goal to see communities reached and transformed by Christ, believing that those who live in the city and are poor can be empowered to live in the freedom, wholeness, and justice of the Kingdom of God fleshed out in local churches and viable urban church planting movements. All our vision, prayer, and efforts are concentrated on a particular social group, the "urban poor," and our commitment to "empower" them through all facets of our work.

While the phrase "the urban poor" may be misunderstood or misused, we have chosen to employ it with our own stipulated meanings, informed by biblical theology as well as urban sociology. We employ the term to identify those whom God has commissioned us to serve, as well as to represent God's prophetic call to proclaim Good News to the poor, both to the church and to our society at large.

It must be conceded, of course, that the term "urban poor" may be easily misapplied and misused. The American city is dramatically diverse, profoundly complex in its mixtures of classes, cultures, and ethnicities. Amid so much diversity, a phrase like "the urban poor" may, at first glance, appear to be too denotative to be suitable as a summary designation of those whom we serve, being somewhat dry and academic. Without clearly stipulating what you mean when you use it, it can easily turn to mere labeling, which tends to reinforce stereotypes, encouraging generalizations about city dwellers which are either too vague or generic to be useful.

Further, some might even suggest that such language is used for its sensationalized impact, for "tear jerk" effect, largely used to illicit donor response without providing clear information on a particular communities or grouping. It is argued that language like "urban poor"

Context
Values/Vision
Prepare
Launch
Assemble
Nurture
Transition
Schedule/Charter

Source:
Ripe for Harvest,
pp. 195-200

encourages over-generalization, and, using such terms to describe thousands, even millions of discrete cultures and communities is demeaning, sloppy thinking, and generally belittling to urban folk. Others suggest that such terms as "urban poor" should be replaced with other terms more sensitive to urban people, suggesting alternative phrases as "the disenfranchised" or "the economically oppressed." Some might even suggest that using any language that asserts particular differences between and among urban dwellers on the basis of class is inappropriate, and unnecessarily creates division among those whom Christ died for.

While these and related arguments have some validity, especially for those who use phrases like this in an insensitive and unthinking manner, none of them, either separate or together, disqualify the legitimate use of that term. For more than four decades as a national missions organization, World Impact has boldly identified its target population as those who reside in the city who are socio-economically poor. We use the language of "the urban poor" in this light, informed by the demographics in the city and the teaching of the Scriptures regarding God's commitment to the poor.

Poverty in the United States continues to rise. In data gathered as late as 2010, the poverty rate has been increasing to 15.1 percent in 2010 from 14.3 percent in 2009 and 13.2 percent in 2008. According to the research think-tank, the Urban Institute, there were 46.2 million poor people in 2010 compared to 43.2 million in 2009, with the poverty rater looming higher than it has been since 1993 (Urban Institute, Unemployment and Recovery Project, September 13. 2011). Sluggish job markets, high unemployment, and rising poverty rates have dramatically impacted urban communities, with literally thousands of families lacking income and access to the basic resources to live and survive. World Impact unashamedly focuses its time and attention on evangelizing, equipping, and empowering those in communities hardest hit by our recessions, economic blight, and all the by-products of violence, crime, broken family, and the overall desperation that poverty and hopelessness brings.

We do not use the term "urban poor" only to clearly identify the population to which we have been historically called. We also use the term because of the prophetic meaning of the poor in Scripture. Many dozens of text in both Old and New Testaments reveal a consistent perspective regarding God and those who are poor. They show that God has always had a burden for those who lack power, resources, money, or the necessities of life. The standards God gave to his covenant people regarding the poor reveal his commitment to the

Context
Values/Vision
Prepare
Launch
Assemble
Nurture
Transition
Schedule/Charter

Source: *Ripe for Harvest,* pp. 195-200

destitute, and all groups and classes associated with them. It is clear that the Old Testament includes a number of groups in close proximity to the poor, including orphans, widows, slaves, and the oppressed (e.g., Deut. 15; Ruth; Isa. 1). Those who exploited and took advantage of the vulnerable because of their poverty and weakness would be judged, and mercy and kindness was exhorted as the universal standard of God's people on behalf of the poor. The Law provided numerous commands regarding the fair and gracious treatment of the poor and the needy, of the demand to provide the hungry and destitute with food, and for the liberal treatment of the poor (Deut. 15.11).

The New Testament reveals God's heart for the poor crystallized in the incarnation of Jesus. Jesus proclaimed in his inaugural sermon that he was anointed with God's Spirit to proclaim the Good News of the Kingdom to the poor (Luke 4.18; 6.20), and confirmed his Messianic identity to John the Baptizer with preaching to the poor, along with healings and miracles (Luke 7.18-23). The Lord declared Zacchaeus' justice to the poor as a sign of his salvation (Luke 19.8-10), and he identified himself unequivocally with those who were sick, in prison, strangers, hungry, thirsty, and naked (Matt. 25.31-45). Every facet of Jesus' life and ministry intersected with the needs of those who lacked resources and money, and therefore could be easily exploited, oppressed, and taken advantage of.

In the actions and writings of the Apostles, we also see clear statements regarding God's election of and care for those who are economically poor. James 2.5 says that God has chosen the poor in this world to be rich in faith and to inherit the Kingdom he promised to those who love him. Paul told the Corinthians that God has chosen the foolish things of the world to shame the wise, the weak things of the world to shame the strong, the lowly and despised things of this world to nullify the things that are, in order that no one might boast in his presence (1 Cor. 1.27-29). This text and others thicken our view of the poor as merely lacking goods, services, and resources: more than that, the poor are those who need make them vulnerable to the effect of their need and the world's exploitation, and are desperate enough to rely on God's strength alone.

In using the term "urban poor" we make clear both the target population that guides the decisions and outreaches of our ministry, as well as unashamedly testify to the biblical perspective of God's election of and commitment to the most vulnerable, needy, and exposed people within our society. Urban dwellers outnumber all other populations today, and our cities have been magnets for massive migrations of

Context
Values/Vision
Prepare
Launch
Assemble
Nurture
Transition
Schedule/Charter

Source: *Ripe for Harvest*, pp. 195-200

urban peoples looking for economic betterment. We believe that "empowering the urban poor" therefore is missionally strategic and prophetically potent. Missionally, the phrase is strategic because it rightly denotes the vast numbers of people who remain unreached with the Gospel of Christ who dwell in our cities. Prophetically, it is potent because it reveals our bold and unashamed call to follow in the footsteps of Jesus, our respect for the poorest of the poor, our belief that God is calling the poor to be members of his church, and our confidence that the urban poor have a significant place in raising up leaders who will reach the cities of our nation, and beyond.

What of the use of the term "urban poor" and World Impact's prayer partners and donors, and our friends and neighbors in the city? To begin with, we have used the term clearly and circumspectly to help anyone interested in our mission agency know precisely those whom God has called us to reach. We love the families and individuals that we serve in the city, and ought never use language (this phrase or any other) to shame or exploit our relationship with them. We do not use this term as a stereotyping label, some pejorative stamp to limit the potential of the communities where we live and work. Rather, we use the phrase in our materials in order to communicate clearly, forthrightly, and persuasively argue the priority of this long neglected field in evangelical mission. From the beginning we have unashamedly committed our lives and resources to making disciples and planting churches among America's urban poor. This is a stewardship, the outworking of our individual and corporate call as missionaries of Christ. God forbid that any one of us would use such language to denigrate the very ones for whom Christ died, those to whom we are called, and those which we believe are the key to future mission in America, and beyond! Speaking clearly regarding our calling is our duty, which never includes shaming or belittling any person to which we are called. For the sake of our mission, our donors, and those whom we serve, we must be unequivocal regarding our target population; likewise, we must never shame nor denigrate them in our use of any communication, ever.

"Empowering the urban poor," therefore, as our adopted language, is neither just a tag-line nor a catchy motto. Rather, for us it functions as a representation of our single vision, the integrating mission of our work as an interdenominational ministry in the city. We believe that empowerment is neither merely meeting needs, dealing only with the mere symptoms of underlying structures of poverty, nor is it being hegemonic patrons to the poor, making them forever dependent on our charity and service. As missionaries of Christ, we believe that the poor,

Context
Values/Vision
Prepare
Launch
Assemble
Nurture
Transition
Schedule/Charter

Source:
Ripe for Harvest,
pp. 195-200

like any other people, can be redeemed, transformed, and released to be the people of God in their own communities. When God wanted to empower his people, he sent his Holy Spirit upon the apostolic company, and formed a community which he entrusted with the life of God and the Word of life. The answer of God to systemic poverty and neglect was to form a people who embodied the very life of the Kingdom where freedom, wholeness, and justice reside. These communities are entrusted with a mission to gather the elect from among the poorest, most broken people on earth, and, through the power of the Spirit and Christian community, see the Kingdom come to earth in new relationships of hospitality, generosity, and righteousness, right where they live. Every healthy functioning church is an outpost of the Kingdom of God, and can be a place where true transformation takes place. Nothing "empowers" the poor like a simple assembly of believers, obedient to the Lordship of Christ!

Armed with this perspective, we wholeheartedly believe that no organization in the history of the world can recognize the dignity and value of the poor like the Church of Jesus Christ. In light of this conviction, World Impact strives to plant as many churches as fast as possible among the various cultures represented by the urban poor, in all of our cities and beyond. We are convinced that no other social organization has the endorsement of God, the headship of Christ, and the power of the Spirit like a healthy functioning local church. And, nothing empowers a community like facilitating church planting movements among the urban poor, where the life and power of the Gospel of Christ can reach and transform entire communities as outposts of the Kingdom. All that we do in mission and in justice (from our camps, our schools, our businesses, medical and dental clinics, our work in the jails and the prisons, and most important of all, our missionary church planting and leadership development efforts) contribute to this empowerment work. Rather than merely meet needs or serve as patrons to the poor, we believe that the Spirit of God can win them, raise up leaders, empower them to lead, and release them as laborers in their very own communities as ambassadors of Christ. More than being recipients of care, we believe they can receive investment to be God's servant leaders, transformers of their communities and co-laborers in God's Kingdom work.

In conclusion, while the phrase "empowering the urban poor" may be misused and misapplied, we at World Impact wholeheartedly embrace the phrase not only because it clarifies the target population of our mission, but also because it unequivocally states our prophetic call to represent God's unchanging commitment to the most vulnerable and least resourced among us. Let us allow Jesus' challenge given so

Context
Values/Vision
Prepare
Launch
Assemble
Nurture
Transition
Schedule/Charter

Source:
Ripe for Harvest,
pp. 195-200

many centuries ago to continue to be our model and vision of ministry today as we seek to fulfill the Great Commission among the world's urban poor:

> Then the King will say to those on his right, "Come, you who are blessed by my Father, inherit the kingdom prepared for you from the foundation of the world. For I was hungry and you gave me food, I was thirsty and you gave me drink, I was a stranger and you welcomed me, I was naked and you clothed me, I was sick and you visited me, I was in prison and you came to me." Then the righteous will answer him, saying, "Lord, when did we see you hungry and feed you, or thirsty and give you drink? And when did we see you a stranger and welcome you, or naked and clothe you? And when did we see you sick or in prison and visit you?" And the King will answer them, "Truly, I say to you, as you did it to one of the least of these my brothers, you did it to me."
>
> ~ Matthew 25.34-40 (ESV)

Source:
The Evangel Dean Handbook,
pp. 193-200

Our Distinctive
Advancing the Kingdom among the Urban Poor

God Has Chosen the Poor

One does not have to read many pages into the New Testament to discover where the early Church got the idea that the poor were specially chosen by God to receive the Gospel and spread it throughout the earth. Jesus, himself, had announced publicly that he was intentionally preaching the Gospel to the poor (Luke 4.18, Luke 6.20) and even suggested that this action helped demonstrate that he was, indeed, the Messiah (Matt. 11.2-6).

The words "chose" and "chosen" in James 2 and 1 Corinthians 1 come from the Greek word eklégomai which means "giving favor to the chosen subject. . . It involves preference and selection from among many choices." In other contexts, it is used to describe God's choice of the "elect" (Mark 13.20) and Jesus' choosing of his disciples (Luke 6.13).

Building on Jesus' teaching, it is not unusual to find very explicit statements in the Epistles about God's choice of, and expectations for, those who are without power, resources, or money. For example, James teaches:

> Listen, my dear brothers: Has not God chosen those who are poor in the eyes of the world to be rich in faith and to inherit the kingdom he promised those who love him?
>
> ~ James 2.5

In a similar manner, Paul writes:

> But God chose the foolish things of the world to shame the wise; God chose the weak things of the world to shame the strong. He chose the lowly things of this world and the despised things-and the things that are not-to nullify the things that are, so that no one may boast before him.
>
> ~ 1 Corinthians 1.27-29

These ideas are not a new theme introduced by the New Testament writers. Instead, they faithfully reflect the Old Testament teachings about how God relates to the poor. One scholar summarizes the Old Testament teaching about the poor in three principles.

Douglas J. Moo, James, *Tyndale Old Testament Commentary Series,* Gen. Ed. Leon Morris. Leicester, England-Grand Rapids, MI: IVP-Eerdmans, 1985. pp. 53-54.

1. God has a particular concern for the poor.
2. God's people must manifest a similar concern [for the poor].
3. The poor are frequently identified with the pious and the righteous.

Source: *The Evangel Dean Handbook,* pp. 193-200

Who Are the Poor?

> In the teaching of Jesus, material possessions are not regarded as evil, but as dangerous. The poor are often shown to be happier than the rich, because it is easier for them to have an attitude of dependence upon God.
>
> ~ R.E. Nixon. "Poverty." *The Illustrated Bible Dictionary*. eds. J.D. Douglas, et al. Leicester, England: IVP, 1980. p. 1255.

To understand God's choice of the poor it is necessary to understand who the "poor" are. The way that Scripture uses the term "poor" is both alike and different from the way we often use the term.

1. The Greek word used in the New Testament means essentially the same thing as our English word "poor." It describes someone who is economically deprived, someone who doesn't have enough money or resources. However, when this word is used by the New Testament writers, they seem to also rely on the Old Testament understandings of the word "poor." Thus, in the New Testament, the poor are both "those who don't have enough money" (Greek understanding) plus "something else" (the Hebrew understanding).

2. This "something else" was an understanding developed over time in the Hebrew Scriptures. In the Old Testament, "the poor" are those who are so powerless and dependent that they are vulnerable to being misused by those who have influence in the society. The emphasis is on *being on the wrong end of a relationship* with those in power. Therefore, in the Old Testament, the poor came to mean those people who were characterized by three things:

    a. They lack the money and resources they need,

    b. They are taken advantage of by those who do have money and resources, and

    c. The result is that they must humbly turn to God as their only source of protection.

3. Therefore, from a theological point of view, we could say that Scripture defines "the poor" as:

Source: *The Evangel Dean Handbook*, pp. 193-200

Those whose need makes them desperate enough to rely on God alone.

Biblical scholar Robert A. Guelich makes exactly these points when he writes about the development of the term "poor" in the Old Testament.

> The most common of these words [for the poor], *'ny* and its later relative, *'nw*, have a much broader scope than simply to denote a socioeconomic status. . . . The *'ny* refers to one so powerless and dependent as to be vulnerable to exploitation by those who have the power base. Thus the accent falls on a socioeconomic relationship rather than on material possessions as such. Yet this powerless and dependent relationship caused one to rely upon God for one's needs and vindication. This humble posture of the poor devoid of pretension before God reflects the religious dimension and comes out frequently in the Psalms. . . . But the religious dimension is never exclusive of the socioeconomic. Both elements are integral to *'ny*. . . . .In summary, the poor in Judaism referred to those in desperate need (socioeconomic element) whose helplessness drove them to a dependent relationship with God (religious element) for the supplying of their needs and their vindication.
>
> ~ Robert A. Guelich. *The Sermon on the Mount*. Waco: Word Books, 1982. pp. 68-69.

This understanding helps us perceive how Luke can record Jesus' teaching as "Blessed are *the poor* for yours is the Kingdom of God" (Luke 6.20); while Matthew records "Blessed are the *poor in spirit* for theirs is the Kingdom of heaven" (Matt. 5.3). In both accounts the point is the same: blessed are those who have become desperate enough to rely on God alone. Only people who are willing to acknowledge their helplessness can receive this help from God. As Clarence Jordan points out:

> When one says 'I don't need to be poor in things; I'm poor in spirit,' and another says, 'I don't need to be poor in spirit; I'm poor in things,' both are justifying themselves as they are, and are saying in unison, 'I don't need.' With that cry on his lips, no man can repent.
>
> ~ Clarence Jordan. *Sermon on the Mount*, Rev. ed. Valley Forge: Koinonia-Judson Press, 1980. p. 20.

Obviously, people who are not poor can come to this point of being desperate enough to rely on God alone. (The Bible records many examples, such as Zaccheus or Joseph of Arimathea, to make this

What are some life experiences besides poverty that often help people realize their desperate need for God?

Source: *The Evangel Dean Handbook,* pp. 193-200

apparent.) *It is also clear that many poor people may refuse to acknowledge their need before God.* However, Jesus and the apostles consistently teach that it is even more difficult for the affluent to acknowledge their need for God (Matt. 19.24; Mark 10.23; James 2.6-7) and that the poor should be expected to respond with faith. This confidence in God's choice of the poor is so profound that one scholar can say: "In the New Testament the poor replace Israel as the focus of the gospel" (C.M.N. Sugden, "Poverty and Wealth," *New Dictionary of Theology*, eds. Sinclair B. Ferguson, et al. [Downers Grove: InterVarsity Press, 1988], p. 524).

Four Fundamental Responses

> To live in radical obedience to Jesus Christ means to be identified with the poor and oppressed. If that is not clear in the New Testament, then nothing is.
>
> ~ Jim Wallis. *Agenda for Biblical People.* New York: Harper & Row, 1976. p. 94.

When we recognize that the Scriptures treat the poor as a group with theological significance, it forces us to consider what our response will be. Both as Christians, and as missionaries, there are at least four responses that we should make.

1. Respect

God's choice of the poor fundamentally challenges the normal way that people respond to the poor. Within society, people avoid the poor, disdain their ways, and expect little from them in any area. Certainly they are not seen as the natural place to search for leaders.

God, however, identifies himself with the poor. The Scriptures say that to oppress the poor is to show contempt to God himself (Prov. 14.31). God's identification with the poor and God's choice of the poor (James 2.5) should make a profound difference to anyone who acknowledges Christ as Lord. Simply put:

- If we respect God, we will respect the poor.
- If we obey God, we will identify with the poor.
- If we believe God, we will see the poor as the potential leaders of his Church.

Source: *The Evangel Dean Handbook,* pp. 193-200

Sadly, many people look at those who are poor and see them primarily as objects of benevolence. Such people view the poor only as those who need their help. While it is certainly right to help the poor (see point two below), such help will create dependence and a loss of dignity if it is not firmly coupled with deep respect for the poor as those that God has chosen. We believe it is not a sacrifice, but rather, a privilege and delight to be called to make disciples among the unreached urban poor.

2. Love, Compassion, and Justice

Christians are called to respond to others with love, compassion and justice. This response to the poor is the same response that Christians give to all people everywhere. What makes it unique is that the world system mitigates against applying this concern to the poor. Theologian Thomas C. Oden says:

> Although Christian charity is due everyone, the poor are Christ's particular concern, precisely because they are the neediest.
>
> ~ Thomas C. Oden. *Pastoral Theology: Essentials of Ministry.* San Francisco: Harper & Row, 1983. p. 268.

God emphasizes our response to the poor, not to play favorites, but because otherwise they would be overlooked.

> One of the ways that St. Francis described his relationship with the poor (and others) was through the word "cortesia." We use the word 'courtesy' to mean manners. Originally, it meant the behavior and etiquette expected of one who served at a noble court . . . . For St. Francis . . . cortesia was a way of seeing and acting towards others.
>
> ~ Lawrence Cunningham. *St. Francis of Assisi.* San Francisco: Harper & Row, 1981.

The Scriptures constantly underscore the responsibility of God's people to share with the poor and help them escape from the grinding effects of poverty. God's Word places responsibility on us to work for justice for the poor. Working for shalom (peace, fullness, abundance, wholeness) means that we will never be content to leave the poor to their poverty while any of us have the means to affect change.

Source: *The Evangel Dean Handbook,* pp. 193-200

3. Preach the Gospel

Out of all our responses to the poor, none is more important than preaching the Gospel. It is exactly what Jesus himself did. Nothing is more revolutionary in liberating the poor than bringing them into relationship with God through Christ.

No project or program can ever achieve what salvation does for the poor. In coming to acknowledge Jesus as Lord and Savior, the poor experience radical liberation through the acquisition of an entirely new identity.

- They move from being at the bottom of the social structure to being an adopted child of the King of kings.
- God's favor, protection, and resources are made available through Christ.
- They are given authority over sin, hell, and death, and every evil thing that would seek to destroy them.
- They are incorporated into a new community (the Church) which offers equality, respect, love, sharing, fellowship, and the opportunity to exercise their gifts and calling from God.

Salvation means that the presence of the living God is active among the poor bringing freedom, wholeness, and justice. It means that they are now part of a "royal priesthood," "members of a holy nation," in which they serve as "Christ's ambassadors" announcing hope and reconciliation to those around them who have not yet experienced liberation.

4. Expect Great Things

There is, perhaps, no more surprising statement that comes from Jesus' lips than the word he gives to his disciples in John 14.12-14:

> I tell you the truth, anyone who has faith in me will do what I have been doing. He will do even greater things than these, because I am going to the Father. And I will do whatever you ask in my name, so that the Son may bring glory to the Father. You may ask for anything in my name, and I will do it.

Source:
The Evangel Dean Handbook,
pp. 193-200

> The intercession of a poor man is acceptable and influential wit
>
> ~ The Pastor of Hermas. Bk. 3. *Ante-Nicene Fathers,*
> Eds. A. Roberts and J. Don
> Peabody: Hendrickson, 1995. p. 32.

On the surface, the idea of accomplishing greater things than Jesus seems absurd. And yet, in just a few short years the Book of Acts records more conversions than ever happened within the life and ministry of Jesus.

Two principles underlie this amazing statement. First, Jesus said discipleship reproduces students who are like him (Luke 6.40). Second, when Jesus returned to the Father and sent the Holy Spirit (John 14.16; Acts 2.38), he made his power universally available to all who believe (John 14.14).

It would be easy to expect little from the poor because of their lack of resources. However, when Scripture disciplines our thinking, a new dynamic emerges. We expect congregations of the urban poor to do greater works than Jesus did on earth because they enter into a discipling relationship with Jesus who freely gives them his Holy Spirit.

As we plant churches we must:

- ***Encourage the poor to believe in the calling, gifts, and abilities that God has given them*** (both individually and corporately). We must have faith in what God will do through them even before they believe it themselves.
- ***Set high standards.*** The only acceptable goal for any Christian is to become like Jesus. Being poor is never an excuse for ignoring God's commands or shirking the responsibilities he gives every believer.
- ***Teach people to rely on Jesus, not on us.*** Missionary resources are limited. God's resources are unlimited.
- ***Instill a passion for reproduction*** (evangelism, follow-up, discipleship, and church planting). "You did not choose me, but I chose you to go and bear fruit – fruit that will last. Then the Father will give you whatever you ask in my name" (John 15.16).

Source:
The Evangel Dean Handbook,
pp. 193-200

One veteran missionary, who has served in both U.S. and Brazilian cities, describes successful churches among the urban poor in this manner:

> Churches . . . that used a "we-help-you-in-your-need" methodology were not winning the lower, working class. People were helped but the spiritual direction of their lives did not change . . . . [whereas] churches that lacked financial and earthly resources were filled with poor people, were led by barely literate lay preachers, and made hard demands on people. New members were expected to be faithful tithers, to wear clothes that conformed to a rigid dress code, to carry their Bibles to church, and to dedicate a large amount of time to worship services, healing services, home prayer meetings, street meetings, and outreach visitation. The churches that gave the most and expected the least were not growing, but those that gave the least material benefit and demanded the most were growing fastest. They demanded conversion from sin and preached that Christ had the power to make it happen, and that this power could be received though faith and prayer.
>
> ~ Charles D. Uken. "Discipling White, Blue-Collar Workers and Their Families." *Discipling the City: A Comprehensive Approach to Urban Mission*, 2nd ed. Ed. Roger S. Greenway. Grand Rapids: Baker Book House, 1992. p. 180.

We honor both God and the poor when we respect them enough to believe that they will function as full-fledged disciples of Jesus Christ.

Interaction of Class, Culture, and Race

World Impact, Inc.

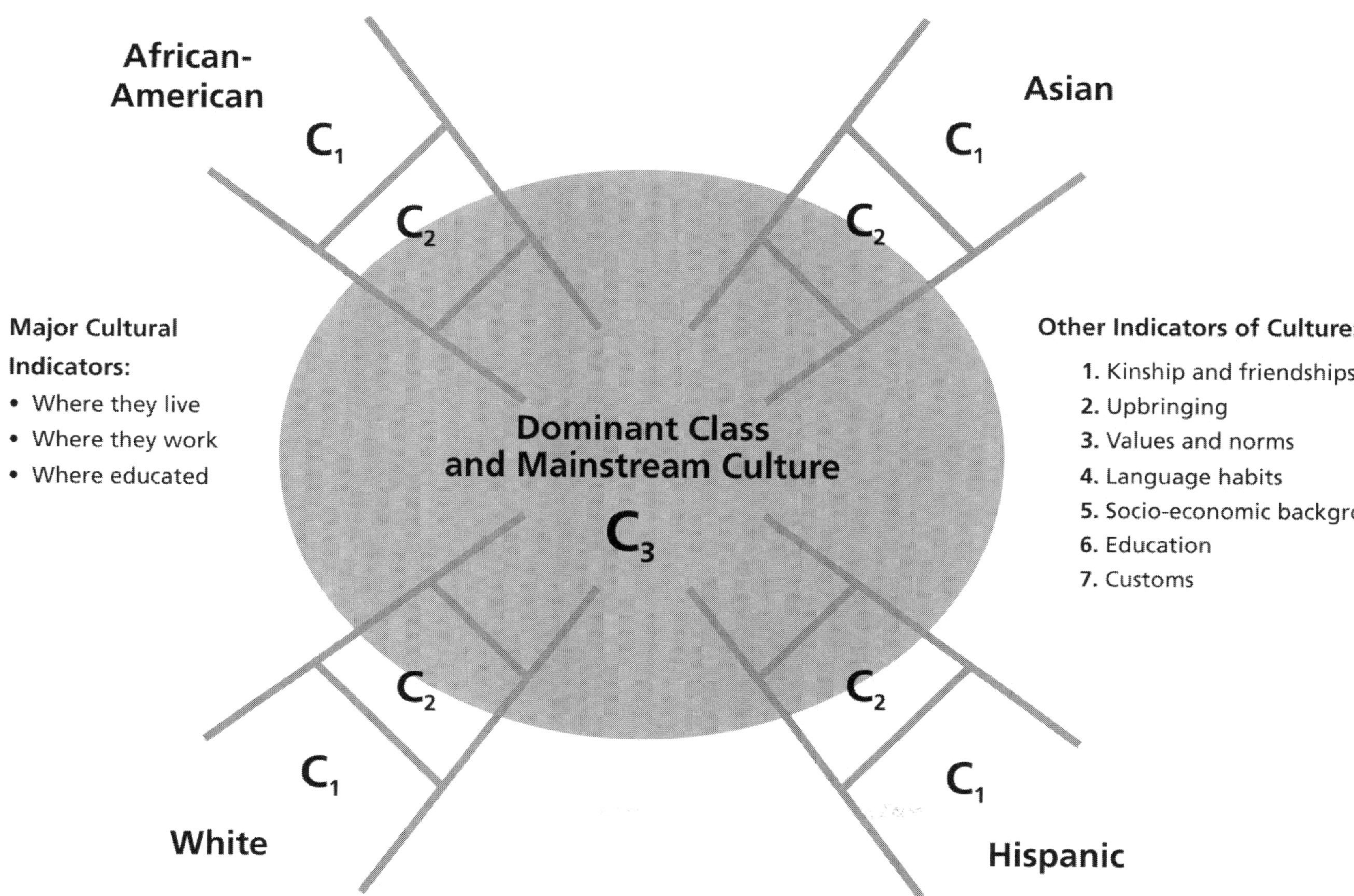

Source: *Planting Churches among the City's Poor, Volume 1*, p. 232

Targeting Unreached Groups in Churched Neighborhoods

Mission Frontiers

Many different peoples!

Many homogenous congregations.

The extent of normal "outreach": Incorporating and gathering according to culture.

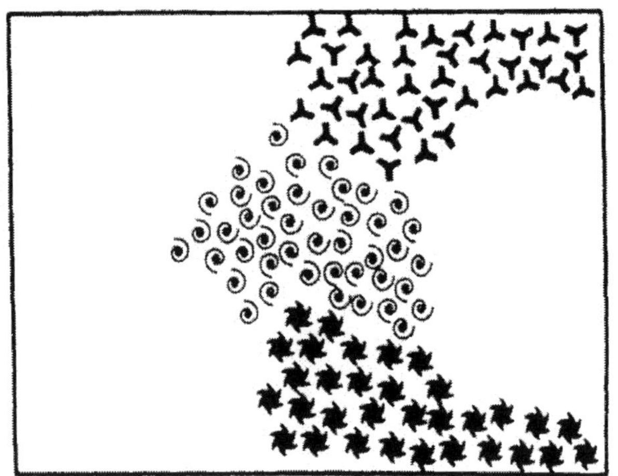

"So close and yet so far away": The unreached, unaffected neighbors.

Source: *Planting Churches among the City's Poor, Volume 1*, p. 256

Source:
Planting Churches among the City's Poor, Volume 1,
pp. 114-118

The SIAFU Network – Assembling God's Warriors
Toward a Strategy to Win the City

> Listen, my beloved brothers, has not God chosen those who are poor in the world to be rich in faith and heirs of the kingdom, which he has promised to those who love him?
>
> ~ James 2.5

If you are an urban Christian, you are caught up in a great battle, a single conflict which is part of a larger war. Yes, the universe is at war, with everything in creation at stake. The opposing forces are disciplined and committed, and in the end, there can only be a single victor. Believe it or not, understand it or ignore it, you still have a role in one of the greatest spiritual struggles in the history of humankind. With hundreds of millions of souls in play, we must each decide whose side we will fight on in this, the campaign of our time.

This motif of spiritual war is prominent throughout the Holy Scriptures, which tell the story of God's commitment to rescue creation from the tyranny of the devil, to save humankind from the penalty and power of sin, and to call together a people from the nations who would belong to him through Christ, his Son. Our God is a man of war (Exod. 15.1-4), a great Lord who promised to send his Son who would be Champion for humankind and all creation, reconciling all things to himself, and establishing his reign in the earth.

We know that Jesus of Nazareth was this promised Champion, who through his incarnation, death, resurrection, ascension, session, and return will accomplish God's rule, including over the dark cities of our time. This basic biblical theology, this faith, is often referred to as the Great Tradition, and TUMI's ongoing passion and project is to recover, articulate, and embody God's truthful Story of redemption and restoration of the world that spans from creation to the consummation of all things. This is key to understanding what God is doing in the world, and central to knowing how we are to live as disciples of Christ in the city today.

The Bible tells the Story of God's determination to restore his kingdom rule, anchored in his loving-kindness and covenantal faithfulness. The Lord God is determined to restore his creation and save out of all humankind a people of his own possession forever. God's Story is authoritatively told in the Scriptures inspired by the Holy Spirit. The

Source: *Planting Churches among the City's Poor, Volume 1,* pp. 114-118

same Scriptures which reveal God's kingdom purpose through the covenants to the Patriarchs lay out in detail the history of Israel, the person and work of Jesus Christ, and his Church.

Since the coming of the Holy Spirit, this Story of rescue and restoration has been cherished, celebrated, and guarded by the Church through the ages, the people of God, in whose life and faith the Story continues to be told, enacted, and expressed. In all aspects of our life together – our theology and worship, our spirituality and discipleship, and our service and mission – the Story of God's glory and grace is embodied in us as witness to the world. We are players in the drama of God, a drama that is being acted out in the streets and neighborhoods of America's inner cities.

Facing a Great Need: The Inner Cities of America

At first glance, the cities of America (and the world) appear to be in trouble, even to be left out of God's drama. Violence, crime, broken families, and despair haunt their streets and neighborhoods, with little hope of change or rescue. Even many Christians have given up, raising the white flag of resignation over the cities of the world, surrendering them to the control of the enemy. Long-term despair and doubt about what God can do in the cities have many believers consigning the cities to the control of the enemy, practically turning those who dwell in them over to those dark forces which prey on the vulnerable and neglected.

Yet, Jesus declared that the gates of hell would not prevail against his church (Matt. 16.18). Our cities can be won, healed, and transformed – all we need is for the brothers and sisters to unite in common purpose for Christ!

The need of the hour for the mean cities of America and the world is clear and plain. We must recruit every godly urban Christian to make themselves available to the Spirit in a new way. As warriors of the Holy Spirit, we must strive with every ounce of our being to mobilize urban disciples into a national community, a common brotherhood and sisterhood who share the same longings, experiences, and dreams as they represent Christ in the cities where they live! Everyone must be mobilized, outfitted, and deployed for service. No one, however young or old, can afford to sit idly on the sidelines during this stark and difficult battle. This is the time for urban churches, urban Christians, and urban leaders to redouble their efforts in the fight, and for everyone, regardless of their status or station in the Church, to report for duty to advance the Kingdom of God. This is the moment of our lives to stand, and to be counted for the Lord!

Source: *Planting Churches among the City's Poor, Volume 1,* pp. 114-118

The SIAFU Network (pronounced see-AH-foo) is a practical means to enable urban disciples to stand together for Christ in the city!

Forming a Great Army: The SIAFU Network

We adopted the siafu ant as our model for the network. The writer of Proverbs spoke of the wisdom and ingenuity of ants who, as they worked together, could accomplish great things for themselves. "Go to the ant, O sluggard; consider her ways, and be wise. Without having any chief, officer, or ruler, she prepares her bread in summer and gathers her food in harvest" (Prov. 6.6-8). Although small and vulnerable as single creatures, they become a mighty and fearsome army when they stand together as one!

> The SIAFU Network is a national association of Chapters anchored in local urban churches, organizations, and/or ministries specifically designed to identify, equip and release spiritually qualified urban servant-leaders to reach and transform the poorest unreached communities in urban America.

The mission of the SIAFU Network is to establish a viable, effective network of urban Christian men and women whose goal is to inspire each other to take full responsibility for one another's lives and well-being, for their marriages and families, for their churches and congregations, and for their communities to advance the Kingdom of Christ in the city.

Our desire is to empower urban Christians to both befriend and mentor one another in order to equip each other to evangelize our unchurched family members and friends, to follow up and disciple new Christians to live the Christian life, and to serve as faithful stewards and servants in our respective Christian churches as outposts of the Kingdom where God has placed them. We also hope to collaborate together in order to identify, train, and release godly, spiritually qualified laborers who can plant churches and help spawn church planting movements which will target the unreached urban neighborhoods of America.

Why the Name *SIAFU*?

The name for this new and exciting collaboration of urban Christians is taken from the example of the African siafu ant community, hailed by the Discovery Channel as the world's fiercest and mightiest social community. A powerful example of community builders, their nests can hold up to twenty-two million members, making them the world's largest social community and easily one of the most productive,

Source: *Planting Churches among the City's Poor, Volume 1,* pp. 114-118

inventive, and remarkable groups ever. Siafu are small, vulnerable, and pesky, easily overcome if you attack or seek to destroy one of them isolated and alone, as a mere individual.

However, when banded together in common unity for the single purpose of the survival and strengthening of the community, they are virtually invincible, taking down all kinds of different animals from goats to buffalo, and (as has sometimes been reported) even elephants in their wake. Their ingenuity and industry (and absolute fierceness) are well known among those who study all the creatures of the insect kingdoms. They are a fitting symbol of the potential that urban Christian men and women possess if they only can unite for the sake of mutual inspiration, edification, equipping, and empowerment. The advancement of the Kingdom of God in America's inner cities lies with urban Christians – identified, inspired, trained, and release for Christ!

Join the Movement:
Consider Forming a Chapter of the SIAFU Network

With so much at stake in Christians answering Christ's call to prophesy and demonstrate deliverance to the cities of America, my heart prayer is that you might consider forming a SIAFU Chapter in your local church or Christian organization. Where two or more disciples gather in the name of Christ, there he is in the midst of them (Matt. 18.20). I am convinced that if we were to mobilize urban disciples of Jesus for the honor and glory of Christ, and for the evangelization and transformation of our neighborhoods, Almighty God will visit us. God has shown in numerous historical contexts that, if his people take him seriously, prepare their hearts for a new move of God, and make themselves available to him to do great things, he can bring revival, renewal, and dramatic change to the city.

Amazingly, all the Lord requires to see this change occur is for his people to prepare themselves for his visitation and remember their shared calling and purpose in the Gospel. Who knows what the Father may accomplish through the millions of urban disciples who currently stand unused and neglected in our cities? What could God do if ordinary urban Christians became united and mobilized under a common purpose to see Jesus exalted in every urban neighborhood in America? We could be on the brink of genuine revival. The tip of the spear of that revival will be mobilized, motivated, and transformed urban disciples standing together for Christ in the city!

Join the SIAFU Network in Order to Win the Lost and Make Disciples

SIAFU activities are specifically designed to help urban disciples bond together in Christ through fellowship, testimony, prayer, and service.

Source: *Planting Churches among the City's Poor, Volume 1,* pp. 114-118

Your Chapter will become a strong, central place to bring seeking souls, to identify emerging servant leaders, to equip hungry disciples for effective ministry, and to evangelize the lost and make disciples in their communities where they live.

Join the SIAFU Network in Order to Strengthen Your Local Church

SIAFU is built on a deep conviction and allegiance to local churches, under the authority of local pastors. Through your Chapter you will create a forum to help you identify and equip your leadership pool in your congregation. Your Chapter will enable them to assemble together, befriend one another, and challenge each other to display their love for Christ through service projects.

Join the SIAFU Network in Order to Touch Your Neighborhood with the Love of Christ

Because we affirm that we were created in Christ for good works (Eph. 2.8-10), SIAFU Chapters select ministry projects to serve and care for others, both inside and outside the church, resulting in real transformation in our communities.

Let us who love the city affirm with all our hearts that God is raising up an army of urban disciples whom he is preparing to mobilize to advance his Kingdom and strengthen his Church. These will undoubtedly be ordinary men and women who love the Lord and their families, who love the Church and the Word, and who look for the return of Christ. God will use common folk who are filled with the Holy Spirit to mobilize an army to declare his praise. Won't you join us, and represent the Kingdom of Jesus with honor, in your neighborhood, where you live? Everything is at stake in you joining this cause. May the Lord lead you as you consider playing your part in the great cosmic drama of our Lord!

The Great Tradition and Creedal Theology

The Story of God: Our Sacred Roots

Rev. Dr. Don L. Davis

The Alpha and the Omega	Christus Victor	Come, Holy Spirit	Your Word Is Truth	The Great Confession	His Life in Us	Living in the Way	Reborn to Serve
The LORD God is the source, sustainer, and end of all things in the heavens and earth. All things were formed and exist by his will and for his eternal glory, the triune God, Father, Son, and Holy Spirit, Rom. 11.36.							
THE TRIUNE GOD'S UNFOLDING DRAMA God's Self-Revelation in Creation, Israel, and Christ				**THE CHURCH'S PARTICIPATION IN GOD'S UNFOLDING DRAMA** Fidelity to the Apostolic Witness to Christ and His Kingdom			
The Objective Foundation: The Sovereign Love of God *God's Narration of His Saving Work in Christ*				**The Subjective Practice: Salvation by Grace through Faith** *The Redeemed's Joyous Response to God's Saving Work in Christ*			
The Author of the Story	*The Champion* of the Story	*The Interpreter* of the Story	*The Testimony* of the Story	*The People* of the Story	*Re-enactment* of the Story	*Embodiment* of the Story	*Continuation* of the Story
The Father as *Director*	Jesus as *Lead Actor*	The Spirit as *Narrator*	Scripture as *Script*	As Saints, *Confessors*	As Worshipers, *Ministers*	As Followers, *Sojourners*	As Servants, *Ambassadors*
Christian *Worldview*	Communal *Identity*	Spiritual *Experience*	Biblical *Authority*	Orthodox *Theology*	Priestly *Worship*	Congregational *Discipleship*	Kingdom *Witness*
Theistic and Trinitarian Vision	Christ-centered Foundation	Spirit-Indwelt and -Filled Community	Canonical and Apostolic Witness	Ancient Creedal Affirmation of Faith	Weekly Gathering in Christian Assembly	Corporate, Ongoing Spiritual Formation	Active Agents of the Reign of God
Sovereign Willing	Messianic Representing	Divine Comforting	Inspired Testifying	Truthful Retelling	Joyful Excelling	Faithful Indwelling	Hopeful Compelling
Creator True Maker of the Cosmos	**Recapitulation** Typos and Fulfillment of the Covenant	**Life-Giver** Regeneration and Adoption	**Divine Inspiration** God-breathed Word	**The Confession of Faith** Union with Christ	**Song and Celebration** Historical Recitation	**Pastoral Oversight** Shepherding the Flock	**Explicit Unity** Love for the Saints
Owner Sovereign Disposer of Creation	**Revealer** Incarnation of the Word	**Teacher** Illuminator of the Truth	**Sacred History** Historical Record	**Baptism into Christ** Communion of Saints	**Homilies and Teachings** Prophetic Proclamation	**Shared Spirituality** Common Journey through the Spiritual Disciplines	**Radical Hospitality** Evidence of God's Kingdom Reign
Ruler Blessed Controller of All Things	**Redeemer** Reconciler of All Things	**Helper** Endowment and the Power	**Biblical Theology** Divine Commentary	**The Rule of Faith** Apostles' Creed and Nicene Creed	**The Lord's Supper** Dramatic Re-enactment	**Embodiment** Anamnesis and Prolepsis through the Church Year	**Extravagant Generosity** Good Works
Covenant Keeper Faithful Promisor	**Restorer** Christ, the Victor over the powers of evil	**Guide** Divine Presence and Shekinah	**Spiritual Food** Sustenance for the Journey	**The Vincentian Canon** Ubiquity, antiquity, universality	**Eschatological Foreshadowing** The Already/Not Yet	**Effective Discipling** Spiritual Formation in the Believing Assembly	**Evangelical Witness** Making Disciples of All People Groups

Source: *Planting Churches among the City's Poor, Volume 1*, p. 195

There Is a River

*Identifying the Streams of a Revitalized Authentic Christian Community in the City**

Rev. Dr. Don L. Davis

Ps. 46.4 (ESV) - There is a river whose streams make glad the city of God, the holy habitation of the Most High.

Tributaries of Authentic Historic Biblical Faith			
Recognized Biblical Identity	**Revived Urban Spirituality**	**Reaffirmed Historical Connectivity**	**Refocused Kingdom Authority**
*The Church Is **One***	*The Church Is **Holy***	*The Church Is **Catholic***	*The Church Is **Apostolic***
A Call to Biblical Fidelity Recognizing the Scriptures as the anchor and foundation of the Christian faith and practice	**A Call to the Freedom, Power, and Fullness of the Holy Spirit** Walking in the holiness, power, gifting, and liberty of the Holy Spirit in the body of Christ	**A Call to Historic Roots and Continuity** Confessing the common historical identity and continuity of authentic Christian faith	**A Call to the Apostolic Faith** Affirming the apostolic tradition as the authoritative ground of the Christian hope
A Call to Messianic Kingdom Identity Rediscovering the story of the promised Messiah and his Kingdom in Jesus of Nazareth	**A Call to Live as Sojourners and Aliens as the People of God** Defining authentic Christian discipleship as faithful membership among God's people	**A Call to Affirm and Express the Global Communion of Saints** Expressing cooperation and collaboration with all other believers, both local and global	**A Call to Representative Authority** Submitting joyfully to God's gifted servants in the Church as undershepherds of true faith
A Call to Creedal Affinity Embracing the Nicene Creed as the shared rule of faith of historic orthodoxy	**A Call to Liturgical, Sacramental, and Catechetical Vitality** Walking in the holiness, power, gifting, and liberty of the Holy Spirit in the body of Christ	**A Call to Radical Hospitality and Good Works** Expressing kingdom love to all, and especially to those of the household of faith	**A Call to Prophetic and Holistic Witness** Proclaiming Christ and his Kingdom in word and deed to our neighbors and all peoples

* This schema is an adaptation and is based on the insights of the *Chicago Call* statement of May 1977, where various leading evangelical scholars and practitioners met to discuss the relationship of modern evangelicalism to the historic Christian faith.

Source: *Planting Churches among the City's Poor, Volume 1*, p. 182

Substitute Centers to a Christ-Centered Vision

Goods and Effects Which Our Culture Substitutes as the Ultimate Concern

Rev. Dr. Don L. Davis

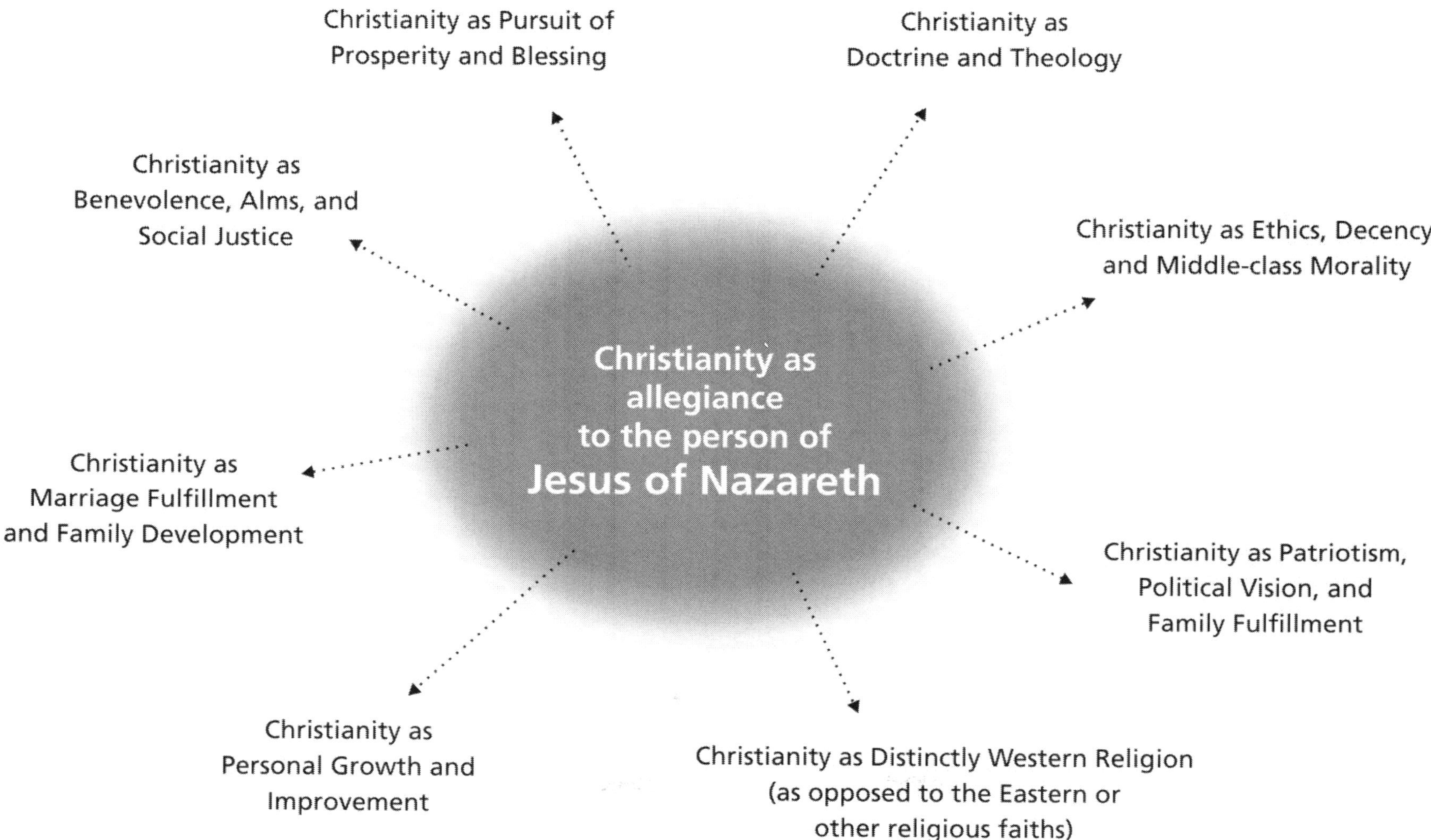

Source: *Planting Churches among the City's Poor, Volume 1*, p. 196

The Picture and the Drama

Image and Story in the Recovery of Biblical Myth

Rev. Dr. Don L. Davis

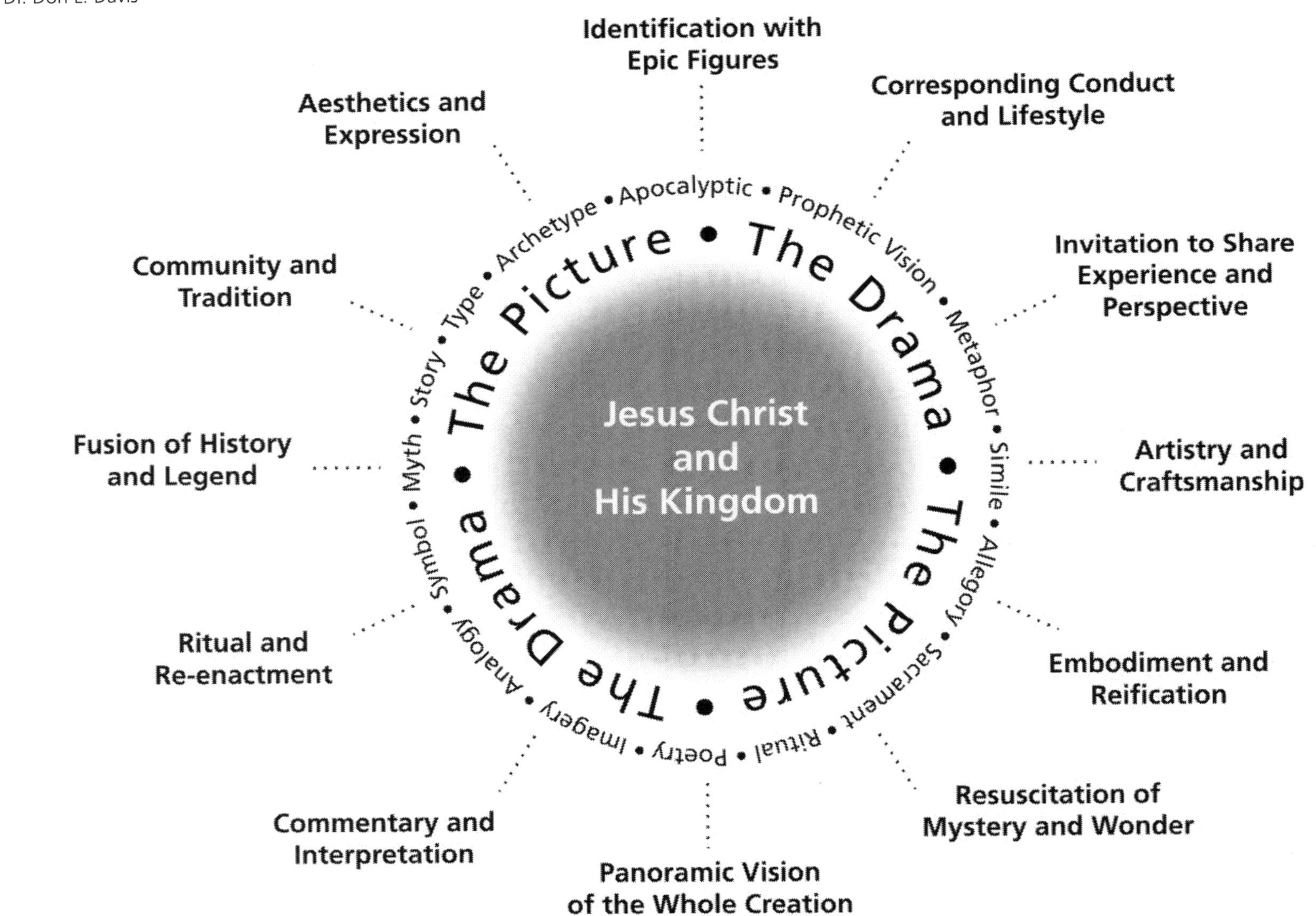

Source: *Planting Churches among the City's Poor, Volume 1*, p. 197

Source: *Planting Churches among the City's Poor, Volume 1,* p. 274

From Before to Beyond Time

The Plan of God and Human History

Adapted from Suzanne de Dietrich. *God's Unfolding Purpose*. Philadelphia: Westminster Press, 1976.

I. Before Time (Eternity Past) 1 Cor. 2.7

A. The Eternal Triune God
B. God's Eternal Purpose
C. The Mystery of Iniquity
D. The Principalities and Powers

II. Beginning of Time (Creation and Fall) Gen. 1.1

A. Creative Word
B. Humanity
C. Fall
D. Reign of Death and First Signs of Grace

III. Unfolding of Time (God's Plan Revealed through Israel) Gal. 3.8

A. Promise (Patriarchs)
B. Exodus and Covenant at Sinai
C. Promised Land
D. The City, the Temple, and the Throne (Prophet, Priest, and King)
E. Exile
F. Remnant

IV. Fullness of Time (Incarnation of the Messiah) Gal. 4.4-5

A. The King Comes to His Kingdom
B. The Present Reality of His Reign
C. The Secret of the Kingdom: the Already and the Not Yet
D. The Crucified King
E. The Risen Lord

V. The Last Times (The Descent of the Holy Spirit) Acts 2.16-18

A. Between the Times: the Church as Foretaste of the Kingdom
B. The Church as Agent of the Kingdom
C. The Conflict Between the Kingdoms of Darkness and Light

VI. The Fulfillment of Time (The Second Coming) Matt. 13.40-43

A. The Return of Christ
B. Judgment
C. The Consummation of His Kingdom

VII. Beyond Time (Eternity Future) 1 Cor. 15.24-28

A. Kingdom Handed Over to God the Father
B. God as All in All

The Theology of Christus Victor

A Christ-Centered Biblical Motif for Integrating and Renewing the Urban Church

Rev. Dr. Don L. Davis

	The Promised Messiah	**The Word Made Flesh**	**The Son of Man**	**The Suffering Servant**	**The Lamb of God**	**The Victorious Conqueror**	**The Reigning Lord in Heaven**	**The Bridegroom and Coming King**
Biblical Framework	Israel's hope of Yahweh's anointed who would redeem his people	In the person of Jesus of Nazareth, the Lord has come to the world	As the promised king and divine Son of Man, Jesus reveals the Father's glory and salvation to the world	As Inaugurator of the Kingdom of God, Jesus demonstrates God's reign present through his words, wonders, and works	As both High Priest and Paschal Lamb, Jesus offers himself to God on our behalf as a sacrifice for sin	In his resurrection from the dead and ascension to God's right hand, Jesus is proclaimed as Victor over the power of sin and death	Now reigning at God's right hand till his enemies are made his footstool, Jesus pours out his benefits on his body	Soon the risen and ascended Lord will return to gather his Bride, the Church, and consummate his work
Scripture References	Isa. 9.6-7 Jer. 23.5-6 Isa. 11.1-10	John 1.14-18 Matt. 1.20-23 Phil. 2.6-8	Matt. 2.1-11 Num. 24.17 Luke 1.78-79	Mark 1.14-15 Matt. 12.25-30 Luke 17.20-21	2 Cor. 5.18-21 Isa. 52-53 John 1.29	Eph. 1.16-23 Phil. 2.5-11 Col. 1.15-20	1 Cor. 15.25 Eph. 4.15-16 Acts. 2.32-36	Rom. 14.7-9 Rev. 5.9-13 1 Thess. 4.13-18
Jesus' History	The pre-incarnate, only begotten Son of God in glory	His conception by the Spirit, and birth to Mary	His manifestation to the Magi and to the world	His teaching, exorcisms, miracles, and mighty works among the people	His suffering, crucifixion, death, and burial	His resurrection, with appearances to his witnesses, and his ascension to the Father	The sending of the Holy Spirit and his gifts, and Christ's session in heaven at the Father's right hand	His soon return from heaven to earth as Lord and Christ: the Second Coming
Description	The biblical promise for the seed of Abraham, the prophet like Moses, the son of David	In the Incarnation, God has come to us; Jesus reveals to humankind the Father's glory in fullness	In Jesus, God has shown his salvation to the entire world, including the Gentiles	In Jesus, the promised Kingdom of God has come visibly to earth, demonstrating his binding of Satan and rescinding the Curse	As God's perfect Lamb, Jesus offers himself up to God as a sin offering on behalf of the entire world	In his resurrection and ascension, Jesus destroyed death, disarmed Satan, and rescinded the Curse	Jesus is installed at the Father's right hand as Head of the Church, Firstborn from the dead, and supreme Lord in heaven	As we labor in his harvest field in the world, so we await Christ's return, the fulfillment of his promise
Church Year	**Advent**	**Christmas**	**Season after Epiphany** Baptism and Transfiguration	**Lent**	**Holy Week** Passion	**Eastertide** Easter, Ascension Day, Pentecost	**Season after Pentecost** Trinity Sunday	**Season after Pentecost** All Saints Day, Reign of Christ the King
	The Coming of Christ	*The Birth of Christ*	*The Manifestation of Christ*	*The Ministry of Christ*	*The Suffering and Death of Christ*	*The Resurrection and Ascension of Christ*	*The Heavenly Session of Christ*	*The Reign of Christ*
Spiritual Formation	As we await his Coming, let us proclaim and affirm the hope of Christ	O Word made flesh, let us every heart prepare him room to dwell	Divine Son of Man, show the nations your salvation and glory	In the person of Christ, the power of the reign of God has come to earth and to the Church	May those who share the Lord's death be resurrected with him	Let us participate by faith in the victory of Christ over the power of sin, Satan, and death	Come, indwell us, Holy Spirit, and empower us to advance Christ's Kingdom in the world	We live and work in expectation of his soon return, seeking to please him in all things

Source: *Planting Churches among the City's Poor, Volume 1*, p. 199

Christus Victor

An Integrated Vision for the Christian Life and Witness

Rev. Dr. Don L. Davis

For the Church

- The Church is the primary extension of Jesus in the world
- Ransomed treasure of the victorious, risen Christ
- *Laos:* The people of God
- God's new creation: presence of the future
- Locus and agent of the Already/Not Yet Kingdom

For Theology and Doctrine

- The authoritative Word of Christ's victory: the Apostolic Tradition: the Holy Scriptures
- Theology as commentary on the grand narrative of God
- *Christus Victor* as the core theological framework for meaning in the world
- The Nicene Creed: the Story of God's triumphant grace

For Spirituality

- The Holy Spirit's presence and power in the midst of God's people
- Sharing in the disciplines of the Spirit
- Gatherings, lectionary, liturgy, and our observances in the Church Year
- Living the life of the risen Christ in the rhythm of our ordinary lives

For Gifts

- God's gracious endowments and benefits from *Christus Victor*
- Pastoral offices to the Church
- The Holy Spirit's sovereign dispensing of the gifts
- Stewardship: divine, diverse gifts for the common good

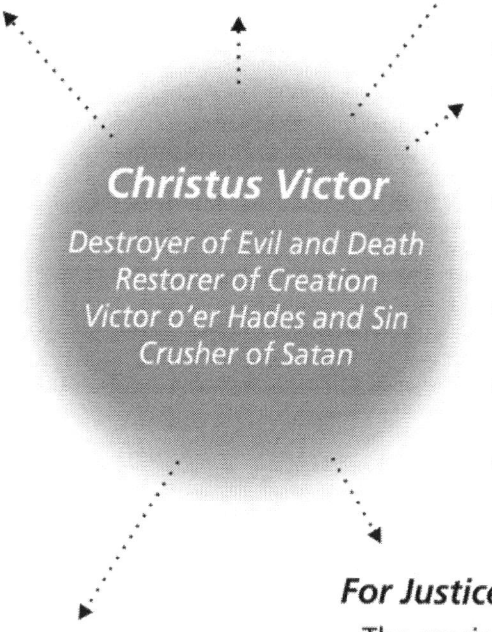

Christus Victor

Destroyer of Evil and Death
Restorer of Creation
Victor o'er Hades and Sin
Crusher of Satan

For Worship

- People of the Resurrection: unending celebration of the people of God
- Remembering, participating in the Christ event in our worship
- Listen and respond to the Word
- Transformed at the Table, the Lord's Supper
- The presence of the Father through the Son in the Spirit

For Evangelism and Mission

- Evangelism as unashamed declaration and demonstration of *Christus Victor* to the world
- The Gospel as Good News of kingdom pledge
- We proclaim God's Kingdom come in the person of Jesus of Nazareth
- The Great Commission: go to all people groups making disciples of Christ and his Kingdom
- Proclaiming Christ as Lord and Messiah

For Justice and Compassion

- The gracious and generous expressions of Jesus through the Church
- The Church displays the very life of the Kingdom
- The Church demonstrates the very life of the Kingdom of heaven right here and now
- Having freely received, we freely give (no sense of merit or pride)
- Justice as tangible evidence of the Kingdom come

Source: *Planting Churches among the City's Poor, Volume 1,* p. 110

Church Planting Models and Strategies

Source:
Ripe for Harvest,
pp. 62-71

Seminar 3

Using Wisdom in Ministry

The PWR Process

Rev. Don Allsman

God Is a Purposeful God

Matt. 28.19 (ESV) – *Go therefore and make disciples of all nations, baptizing them in the name of the Father and of the Son and of the Holy Spirit.*

Acts 1.8 (ESV) – *But you will receive power when the Holy Spirit has come upon you, and you will be my witnesses in Jerusalem, and in all Judea and Samaria, and to the end of the earth.*

Matt. 24.14 (ESV) – *And this gospel of the kingdom will be proclaimed throughout the whole world as a testimony to all nations, and then the end will come.*

John 15.8 (ESV) – *By this my Father is glorified, that you bear much fruit and so prove to be my disciples.*

How Can We Fulfill God's Purpose? Using Wisdom in Ministry

The Dialectic: Wisdom is choosing what is best between viable truths.

Wisdom not ivory tower experience, but found in ***engagement***.

Eph. 5.15-17 (ESV) – *Look carefully then how you walk, not as unwise but as wise, making the best use of the time, because the days are evil. Therefore do not be foolish, but understand what the will of the Lord is.*

Prov. 24.3-6 (ESV) – *By wisdom a house is built, and by understanding it is established; by knowledge the rooms are filled with all precious and pleasant riches. A wise man is full of strength, and a man of knowledge enhances his might, [6] for by wise guidance you can wage your war, and in abundance of counselors there is victory.*

Context
Values/Vision
Prepare
Launch
Assemble
Nurture
Transition
Schedule/Charter

Source: *Ripe for Harvest,* pp. 62-71

Benefits of Using Wisdom in Ministry Tasks

- Clear vision helps everyone clearly see ***if the team is doing well*** or not.
- Clear direction ***minimizes confusion*** giving a sense of confidence and hope.
- Everyone knows ***their assignment***.
- People can decide if they want to stay and ***help fulfill the vision*** or move on to something else. You do not want people on your team who are not supporting the vision. If they stay they will either become inactive or will cause problems.
- ***Wasteful activities*** are minimized (stay focused on vision, not opportunities).
- An environment is created where you can ***say "no" to opportunities*** that do not contribute to the vision.
- Opportunities that contribute to the vision ***can be anticipated*** and recognized quickly. Nehemiah was ready when the opportunity arose to explain his vision to the king.
- Clarity and direction ***minimizes hurting or discouraging the troops.*** Soldiers die from lack of clarity and direction.
- Wisdom demands a balance between ***vision (faith) and reality (prudence).***
- Clear direction inspires people and sets them ***free to innovate.***
- It provides the tools to be pro-active, ***minimizing becoming a "victim of circumstances."***
- The principles can be applied to ***many areas of the team's activities***. Developing a habit of using wisdom will make every activity, large or small, more effective.

Barriers to Using Wisdom in Ministry Tasks

". . . we are not unaware of his schemes" (2 Cor. 2.11)

- **"We've never done it that way before."** God has no use for traditions that block his progress. Just because it has been done a certain way does not indicate it remains a wise option (Acts 10).
- **"We're doing fine."** Apparent (or real) success can keep you from greater fruitfulness (John 15.2).

Source:
Ripe for Harvest,
pp. 62-71

- **"Being organized doesn't allow for the leading of the Holy Spirit."** God had a plan and is working his plan through us. We should not be ashamed to have a plan and work that plan.
- **"It doesn't matter what we do – God will bless it. We will face it when we come to it."** While there are some things that are better left later, sometimes this attitude reflects a lack of discipline.
- **"We can do it" rather than "we should do it."** – basing decisions on emotion, expediency, or available resources.
  - ~ Keep a clear focus on the vision.
  - ~ Engage activities which contribute to that vision.
  - ~ Many good things to invest in, but only a few *contribute to the vision*.
  - ~ Poor stewardship to be driven by opportunities rather than by vision.
  - ~ Wisely consider the implications of decisions, not the easiest path.
  - ~ Emotions can easily deceive us. "Be clear-minded and self-controlled so you can pray" (1 Pet. 4.7).
  - ~ The path of least resistance often carries a price to pay.
  - ~ CONTRIBUTION TO VISION.
- **Fatigue.** "Fatigue makes cowards of us all." When we get tired, we are more resistant to new ideas and anything which will tap our already-low resources. This resistance can result in missed opportunities.
- **Fear of failure, fear of change, fear of losing supporters**
  - ~ Mediocrity is preferable because it is safer.
  - ~ Risk brings the prospect of personal failure and humiliation ("For God gave us a spirit not of fear but of power and love and self-control," 2 Tim. 1.7).
  - ~ Natural to dread change, but we are constantly being transformed (Rom. 12.2; 2 Cor. 3.18).
  - ~ Flexibility (openness to change) is critical to exercising wisdom (God does things we don't expect).
  - ~ Wisdom may dictate action resulting in controversy, but if it is in the best interest of the vision, you must act courageously and sensitively.

Context
Values/Vision
Prepare
Launch
Assemble
Nurture
Transition
Schedule/Charter

Source:
Ripe for Harvest,
pp. 62-71

- **Willingness to be in a protracted conflict**
  - ~ Armies continue fighting even when they know they will be defeated.
  - ~ Prolonging the war reduces the humiliation of defeat.
  - ~ You need help to be victorious but also when to minimize your losses.
  - ~ "Encouraging people to pledge themselves to survival is an admission of defeat" (George Barna).
- **Experience.** "I've been here a long time and I know what's been going on. I've been in this community for twelve years and I know this isn't going to work."

Process that addresses barriers and benefits, and is both deliberate and emergent:

- Deliberate: Decide now, before it's too late.
- Emergent: Face when it comes.

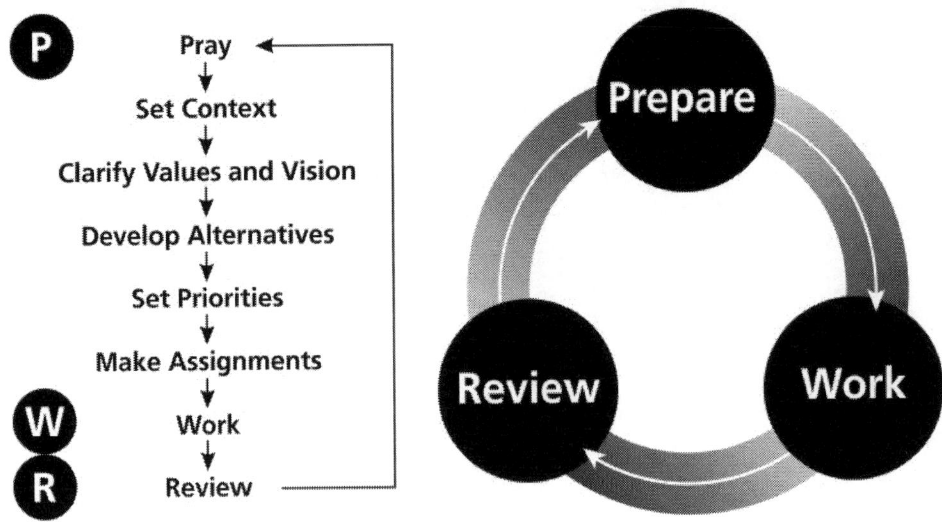

Context
Values/Vision
Prepare
Launch
Assemble
Nurture
Transition
Schedule/Charter

Source: *Ripe for Harvest,* pp. 62-71

PWR

PREPARE

- ***Pray*** (Discover his plan.)

  "We start not with a plan, but a passion. Motion flows from emotion" (Wheatley).

- ***Set context*** (God is God of history.)

  Good decisions are made in the proper context.

  Be reflective. "In everything the prudent acts with knowledge, but a fool flaunts his folly" (Prov. 13.16).

- ***Clarify the values and vision.***

  Values: 3-5 driving forces to find consensus (Abilene Paradox ~ J. Harvey, 1988).

  Who, what, when, how (Great Commission, Moses, Noah, Joshua, Nehemiah).

  Be discerning. "The wisdom of the prudent is to discern his way, but the folly of fools is deceiving" (Prov. 14.8).

- ***Develop alternatives*** (Don't go with the first, most obvious answer.)

  Dream, get counsel.

  Be imaginative. "Plans are established by counsel; by wise guidance wage war" (Prov. 20.18).

- ***Set priorities*** (Don't just try all the alternatives.)

  Be prudent. "The simple believes everything, but the prudent gives thought to his steps. . . . The prudent sees danger and hides himself, but the simple go on and suffer for it" (Prov. 14.15, 22.3).

- ***Make assignments*** (Don't leave people guessing about the specifics of their assignment.)

  Be decisive. ". . . He gave me understanding in all the details of the plan . . . be strong and courageous and do the work" (1 Chron. 28.19-20).

Context
Values/Vision
Prepare
Launch
Assemble
Nurture
Transition
Schedule/Charter

Source:
Ripe for Harvest,
pp. 62-71

WORK (Stop talking and start doing.)

- Be bold; innovate; "Give the boundaries in which people are free to live out their spiritual gift without asking for permission." ~ Bill Easum
- Friction: things seldom go as planned.
- Better to execute a poor plan than poorly execute a great plan.
- *Be creative.* (Matt. 25.14-30).
- Two extremes: rigidity and lack of discipline.

REVIEW (Don't assume what you did was effective.)

- Make half-time adjustments (Sanballat, Cornelius, Gideon, Macedonian vision).
- Check the fruit (John 15.2).
- "The most important part of any mission is the debrief."
- *Be reflective.* "Poverty and disgrace come to him who ignores instruction, but whoever heeds reproof is honored. . . . Whoever ignores instruction despises himself, but he who listens to reproof gains intelligence" (Prov. 13.18; 15.32).
- Celebrate! (Remember Ed Delahanty's 65.4% failure rate.)

What Is PWR?

You will spend much time in preparation, but don't be deceived. No formula or good plan will plant a church; not an analytic process.

Bobby Bowden on blending control with improvisation: "*You may work all week on a game plan, then get four plays into the game and realize the plan's no good. You have to be able to adjust. You have to build flexibility into your people and strategies.*"

Robert McNamara: "*We must first determine what our foreign policy is to be, formulate a military strategy to carry out that policy, then build the military forces to successfully conduct this strategy*" (Failed Vietnam Strategy).

Source:
Ripe for Harvest,
pp. 62-71

PWR Is About	PWR Is Not About
Adapting	Being organized
Wisdom (wisely pursuing vision)	Goals
Adjustment	Checking off tasks
Learning	Planning
Contribution to vision	Calculated analysis
Fruit checking (John 15.2)	Bean counting
Dreaming and scheming	Paperwork
"Rapid assessment and adaptation to a complex and rapidly changing environment that you can't control" ~ John Boy, OODA Loop	Being linear
Prepare, Work, Review	Pain Without Reward

Applications for PWR
Dimensions: leading a choir, leading a worship service, leading a cell group, planning Church Plant School, elder meetings, worship services, retreats, evangelistic events.

PWR is not World Impact; PWR represents biblical principles of wisdom.

Victory is found when:
There is wise preparation
. . . creatively executed under the guidance of the Holy Spirit
. . . and rigorously reviewed.

Source:
Ripe for Harvest,
pp. 62-71

PWR: Prepare

Don Allsman

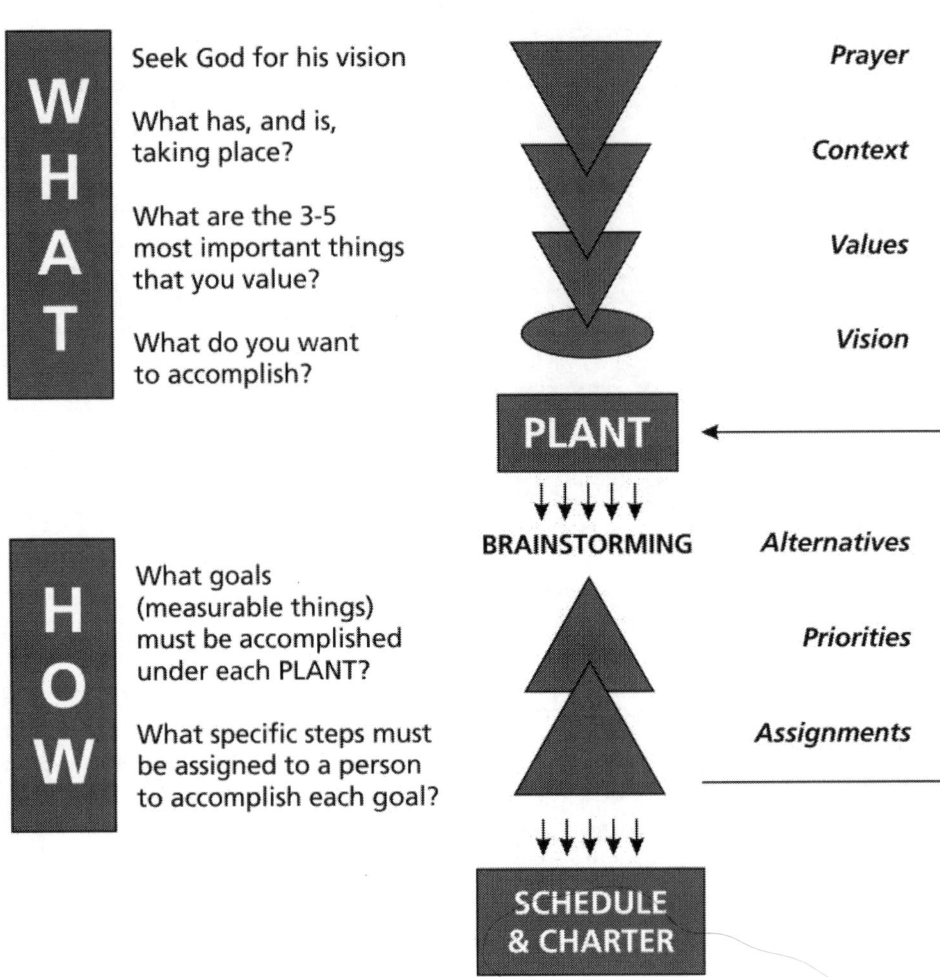

Schedule and Charter
The Charter

End result of the preparation phase of PWR is the charter form

- Captures the entirety of the plan on one sheet
- Helps the team members, the multiple team leader, potential volunteers, and other interested parties see a snapshot of the intentions of the church plant enterprise
- Becomes the means by which the team is given authority, signed off by the Deans, Multiple Team Leader and City Director (World Impact only)

Context
Values/Vision
Prepare
Launch
Assemble
Nurture
Transition
Schedule/Charter

Source: *Ripe for Harvest,* pp. 62-71

No charters are open-ended.

- Due date for charter review
- Review may determine if:
  - ~ an additional length of time should be authorized to continue the effort
  - ~ there is not sufficient fruit from the effort and the team should be disbanded
  - ~ there may need to be wholesale changes in the vision, the team structure, or strategies

The charter makes the team semi-autonomous.

- Allows team to carry out its vision within the stated guidelines without micro-management.
- Creates intensive scrutiny of the team's vision and methods
  - ~ at the front end of charter development
  - ~ at the back end during charter review
- Less scrutiny in the middle during implementation

The charter is the culmination of the strategic planning process and equips the team to proceed with wisdom and authority.

Context
Values/Vision
Prepare
Launch
Assemble
Nurture
Transition
Schedule/Charter

Source:
Ripe for Harvest,
pp. 62-71

Discern God's Vision

Prepare Plan of Attack

Spiritual & Tactical Readiness • Contribution to Vision

Engage the Enemy

Check the Fruit

Prepare New Plan of Attack

- PWR is about wisely ***adapting*** and making ***adjustments***, not organization, goals, or tasks.
- It's about ***learning***, not planning.
- It's about ***vision and fruit checking***, not analysis and bean counting.
- It's about ***dreaming and scheming***, not paperwork.

Source: *Planting Churches among the City's Poor, Volume 2,* pp. 205-206

Davis's Project Gauntlet

The Dirty Dozen Criteria for New Initiatives

Rev. Dr. Don L. Davis

1. Does this project solve a *tough problem*, meet an *urgent need*, or take advantage of a *critical opportunity* faced by urban missionaries, churches, and their leaders? How so?

2. Does this project have *clear sponsors and stakeholders* who are willing to back the project till its completion?

3. Is there some way *to fund this*? What is the likelihood of this initiative adding to our intellectual and financial resources for the immediate and remote future (e.g., doubling or tripling our initial investment in the next 10-12 months)?

4. What would be the makeup of our project team? Do they have *the wherewithal, the expertise, know-how, and experience* to really take on this problem or opportunity?

5. Who would be responsible to create our work breakdown structure for this project, i.e., our definition, tasks, assignments, due dates, etc.? Who will manage this project for us?

6. Are there reasons why we *can't do this*, even if we wanted to? In other words, is this project simply beyond our unique ability to handle? Why or why not?

7. Are there *other strategic project team members* we will need to recruit and underwrite in order to make this happen? Do we have their commitment, and can we fund them?

8. Will this project provide real traction and leverage in our current portfolio as a *critical advantage* project: i.e., would it greatly advance our traction to *multiply churches cross-culturally among the urban poor*, increase our ability to *encourage and resource urban leaders for the urban church through our satellites*, and be *underwritten financially*?

9. Even if we had the money and time to accomplish this right now, do compelling reasons exist that could promote this possibility to *the top echelon of our priorities*? Given the constraints and limits of our time and money issues now, can we afford to put aside other things to work on this? Why?

Source: *Planting Churches among the City's Poor, Volume 2*, pp. 205-206

10. Will we be able to *outsource all or the vast majority of the duplication and production* of the deliverables for this project?

11. Can this project add value and attractiveness to us by being able to *be accessed, distributed, and offered over the web*? Can we integrate its products into our catalog of resources there?

12. The trump of trumps: Do your leaders *authorize* you to do this?

Source:
Planting Churches among the City's Poor, Volume 1, pp. 405-417

Researching Your Community

Rev. Dr. Don L. Davis, expanded, amended, and adapted from *You and Your Community, National Council of Churches*

The following questions were designed in order of a parish or community based church or Christian service/mission organization to study carefully and learn more of the precise nature of the needs and potentials its community possesses. These questions are comprehensive but not exhaustive, and are meant to provoke your mind to explore the various situations, experiences, needs, and critical concerns that are intrinsic to the community where you live, work, and witness. Each broad question area could easily be delegated to a researcher or task force that would investigate this area and present information regarding the community's overall condition.

I. What Area of the City or County Do You Regard as Your Target Community?

1. What does your community call itself?
2. What is the extent and what are the boundaries of your natural geographical parish?
3. What are your community's chief characteristics?
4. What are its traditions, histories, legacies; how did this community come to be, who founded it, when and how?
5. What is the predominant character of it – industrial, commercial, agricultural, educational, recreational, or residential?
6. What are the "natural" boundaries which outline your community, i.e., major streets or highways, railroad lines, parks, industrial or business districts, rivers or bodies of waters, etc.?
7. What is its relationship to its neighboring communities, town/ city at large?
8. What is the general accepted opinion or attitude towards the community and its residents? What is it known/famous for?
9. What is the unit you regard as your community (precinct, ward, village, town, city, county)? What is its total area and population?
10. What is the nature of its adjoining communities? What nearby cities influence the life of your community? (Is it rural, village, urban, suburban)?
11. Describe the various physical characteristics and general well-being or status of your community?

Source: *Planting Churches among the City's Poor, Volume 1*, pp. 405-417

II. Who Lives in Your Community?

1. How many people live within your target area?
2. What is the density of the population, i.e., its socioeconomic, racial, religious, cultural/ethnic, age, gender, educational distribution?
3. What are the differing cultures, races, nationalities, ethnicities represented in your community, and how are they distributed within it? What areas of the community do these differing people groups reside?
4. How long have the majority of residents lived in your community?
5. How fast are your community's residents either moving in or exiting your area?
6. How large are the average family units, and what kind of families make up the majority of homes in the community (single parent, two parent, with or without children, etc.)?
7. What are the current birth and death rates for the community?
8. What are the current rates of divorce, legal separation, broken families, etc.?
9. What are the some the predominant kinship patterns in the community?
10. What percent of the population would be considered "alternative" or even considered as "deviant" by the majority culture's standards (homosexual community, some particular minority community, etc.)?
11. Where did most of the residents come from (where did they live before they moved into the neighborhood)?
12. Where do most people who exit this community go?
13. How do the majority of residents view as their community's strengths and/or weaknesses?
14. How cohesive and unified are the members of the community?

III. What Is the Character of the Housing Within the Community?

1. What percentage of the families or individuals own or lease their home?
2. What do these homes cost and/or what is the average rental fee?
3. Who are the land and property owners for most of the community?
4. What is the general condition of the rental housing in the community?

Source: *Planting Churches among the City's Poor, Volume 1*, pp. 405-417

5. To what extent is the property adequately repaired and maintained? Why?
6. How many of the residents of the community lack adequate housing? What is the number of homeless people in this neighborhood?
7. How many hotels, rooming houses, trailer camps, and other facilities exist for transients and the homeless?
8. How does the housing opportunities in your neighborhood compare to dwellings in neighboring communities?
9. Who are the individuals in charge of public housing administration in this area? Who are the key Realtors and realty agencies here?
10. What is the number of government units and housing in the area? Are there any government housing projects? If so, how many currently live in these homes/apartments/duplexes?
11. What are the current building projects taking place in the community that have the potential to change the current housing situation?
12. What innovate housing alternatives exist for the poor and needy in this area?
13. According to population trends, what will the community need in obtain or change in light of its future housing needs?

IV. What Is the Economic Condition and Character of the Community?

1. What is the income range of the people in our community? What tax brackets are represented within it?
2. How do most of its residents earn their living?
3. What percentage of the communities working population commute outside of the community to work?
4. What percentage of community residents are unemployed? Stratify your answer according to population differences in race, gender, ethnicity, education level, etc.
5. What is the standard of living in the community compared to other communities nearby, and the city at large?
6. What opportunities and/or problems do most residents encounter in finding or maintaining employment?
7. Are commercial interests running high here? Why or why not?

Source: *Planting Churches among the City's Poor, Volume 1,* pp. 405-417

8. How do entrepreneurs or other financial investors see this community? Have the banks redlined this area, or which banks are offering money to its residents for business, home, and other financial opportunities?
9. What is the relationship of the community to the overall business community in the city (e.g., the Rotary club, the Chamber of Commerce, Business groups, etc.)?
10. Who are the key economic and business leaders in the community? What are their assets and key economic enterprises?
11. How much illegal activity (drugs, gambling, prostitution, etc.) takes places in the community, and how do these activities affect the community financially?
12. Are there any examples of blatant economic injustices within the community? If so, how did they arise and what groups or events are responsible?
13. Are there any locally based economic groups seeking to bring renewal to this community? Who are they and what kind of projects are they engaged in?
14. What special hardships have affected the community's economic condition adversely, or what special opportunities have affected it positively in the last 5 years?
15. What do the leading economic indicators show for the economic future of the community?
16. What kind of industries or businesses exist within or border the community (e.g., grocery stores, convenience, fast-food, offices, malls, government, construction, etc.)? What are the major employers, businesses, or industries within the community?

V. What Is the Quality of Education Provided to Your Residents?

1. How many of the residents within your community boundary are of school age?
2. What is the average amount of schooling most adults have in the community? Where were most of the community's residents educated?
3. What are the literacy rates for the adults in the community?
4. What are the major schools in the area (e.g., preschools, grammar schools, middle schools, secondary schools, trade or vocational schools, colleges, institutes, etc.)?

Source: *Planting Churches among the City's Poor, Volume 1,* pp. 405-417

5. How old and in what condition are the various educational institutions in the area?
6. What caliber of teachers are employed in the various levels here, and what sort of facilities are provided at institutions within this community?
7. How do students of various grades rank academically with neighboring communities, in the city or town at-large, and nationally?
8. What are the current teacher-student ratios in the schools at present? What is the level of expertise and experience for the average administrators in the various educational institutions?
9. Who are the key individuals in charge of the administration of the schools at the various levels in the community? Who are the members of the school board and what has been their performance of late?
10. What is the current dropout/truancy rate for the various schools?
11. What is the overall character of the schools, that is, their safety, cleanliness, organization, support? What are the best/worst schools in the community?
12. What teacher or parent-teacher organizations exist that are making an impact on the quality of the education provided in the schools?
13. To what degree is equal privileges open to all children and adults of the area?
14. How many of the communities high school graduates go on to college? What kind of colleges or advanced institutions do they attend?
15. What opportunities exist for remedial or continuing education for adults and young people after they leave high school?

VI. How Is the Community Organized and Governed Politically?

1. How many of the community are of voting age? What percentage of the community typically participates in local and national referendums and voting?
2. How is the local community organized politically? What are the precincts, districts, or zoning sections set up?
3. How many representative slots does the community have on the city council, state government, and national political bodies? Who is responsible for drawing up these districts?

Source: *Planting Churches among the City's Poor, Volume 1,* pp. 405-417

4. Who are the current officials representing the community locally, statewide, and nationally (aldermen, city council members, state representatives, state senators, congressional persons, senators)? How involved/informed have they been of the community's needs and potentials?
5. Who are the civic leaders for the community?
6. What are the organizations and/or institutions that have been associated with resisting injustice and inequality within the community? What are the premier advocacy organizations in the community, and who are their leaders?
7. What are the key political action groups or committees within the community? Who is in charge of these groups and what are their political agendas for the community?
8. How much of the cities resources and goods (dollars, personnel, projects, urban improvements, street maintenance, public services, etc.) have been allocated to this community, and how have those allocated resources been spent and distributed within it? Who are the liaisons serving as "middle-persons" in charge of this distribution?
9. What are the primary political affiliations of the residents within the community? What is the political history of the affiliation of the community at-large?

VII. How Does the Community Dispense Justice by the Law and the Courts?

1. How do most residents describe the status of law enforcement and the administration of justice in the community?
2. Who are the current leaders in the administration of justice in the community (Chief ofpolice, District attorney, etc.)?
3. What courts are located within the community? Who are the key public prosecutors and judges within the community? What is their record regarding the protection of the community and enforcement of the law on behalf of the community?
4. What are the latest statistics regarding the numbers and types of crimes committed within the community, and/or delinquency?
5. What are the numbers of residents currently being incarcerated in city, state, and federal jails or prisons?
6. What provision is made for the treatment and rehabilitation of offenders? What level of provision has been made regarding the offenders families during the incarceration of the offenders?

Source:
Planting Churches among the City's Poor, Volume 1, pp. 405-417

7. What level and caliber of legal representation is provided for and offered to residents of the community? Who are the key attorneys in the community?
8. How many police and city law enforcement officers are assigned to the community for its service and protection?
9. What is the current relationship of the police department to the residents in the community? What steps have been taken to strengthen community-police relations?
10. To what degree have the courts protected the civil rights and liberties of the people in the community?

VIII. What Is the State of the Community's Health and Health Providing Services?

1. How do local health providing institutions characterize the general status of your community's health?
2. Who gets sick most in the community, and why?
3. What are the birth and death rates per thousand? How does this number compare to neighboring communities, the city, and the nation?
4. What are the clinics, hospitals, and medical facilities located in the community? What are the current number of physicians, dentists, specialists, and other medical personnel per capita?
5. Who are the key physicians and care providers in the community?
6. What is the price and quality of care at these various hospitals and clinics in the community?
7. How is the community staffed in terms of ambulance, paramedical, and fire department protection? In other words, how many of these units are assigned to the community? How do the numbers in the community compare with the services used by other communities or the city at large?
8. Who is the fire chief in the community, and who are the key fire prevention officials in the community?
9. What provision has been made in the community for its vulnerable populations, i.e., the elderly, the disabled, the poor and indigent, the mentally retarded, the mentally ill, etc.? Do these populations have access to this provision?

Source: *Planting Churches among the City's Poor, Volume 1*, pp. 405-417

10. What kind of services does the community provide for those who have either been victims of abuse (e.g., children, battered women), or those struggling with addictions (e.g., alcoholism, drugs)? What are the half-way houses or community placement homes available for those in need of such care?
11. What is currently being done in terms of illegitimacy and issues surrounding family planning and care in the community?
12. What provision is being made for the lowering the numbers of people exposed to contagious disease, especially STD's and the AIDS virus?
13. What (if any) are special medical needs or problems confronted by the community? Who has been placed in charge of alleviating these problems, and what is their current rate of success in doing so?
14. What sort of programs exist for the education of the general public regarding safety and health issues in the community?

IX. How Do People Recreate and Spend Their Leisure in the Community?

1. What recreational facilities, hangouts, or spots exist in the community (parks, zoos, pedestrian malls, exercise facilities, music places, clubs, public swimming pools, bowing alleys, sports complexes, etc.)? What are the key commercial amusement centers in the community?
2. Who frequents these various places? Do certain members of the community tend to frequent only special places of interest?
3. What places of recreation or association are not necessarily wholesome or are associated with problem or delinquent activity in the community?
4. What needs does the community have in terms of providing acceptable entertainment under wholesome conditions for its residents, especially its youth?
5. Are the more wholesome places of recreation accessible to all members of the community?
6. Is there sufficient variety and opportunity for play and leisure for all age groups within the community?
7. What is the condition and availability of the parks and public places in the community?

Source: *Planting Churches among the City's Poor, Volume 1,* pp. 405-417

8. What social activities/organizations exist organized either as women's or men's groups, youth groups, groups organized on the basis of age or hobbies or other similar interests?
9. What are the key activities that teens and children participate in during their spare time?
10. What kinds of festivals, traditional meetings, parades, or celebrations does the community participate in each year?
11. What music groups, bands, drama and theater groups, or cultural groups (poets, sculptors, artists) exist and are well known within the community?
12. What kind of sports leagues exist for the community's participation?
13. What kinds of activities and resources are available to the community in its various community centers (Boys or Girls clubs, Boys Scouts or Girl Scouts, YMCA, etc.)?

X. What Are the Key Media Centers Based within the Community?

1. What are the key community voices of media present (newspapers, newsletters, radio stations, television stations, publishing centers, etc.)? Who owns these and what are their circulation and audience numbers?
2. Who are the key persons consulted by the media as spokespersons for the community?
3. What are the key organizations, individuals, or institutions within the community that give voice to its opinions, views, and positions?
4. How does the media depict the community – what issues, themes, stories, personalities does the media tend focus upon in its analysis of the community?
5. What kinds of community programming is made available for the community's discretion on radio and television?
6. Who are the reporters or journalists assigned to deal with issues related to the needs and life of the community?
7. What neighborhood-based community newspapers or newsletters address the particular concerns of members of the community? Who owns them? How often are they published, and how great is their staffs?

Source:
Planting Churches among the City's Poor, Volume 1, pp. 405-417

XI. How Does the Community Address Its Residents with Special Needs?

1. What are the most vulnerable populations in the community right now?
2. What level of awareness exists regarding these populations among its residents, its leaders, its care providers, etc.?
3. What are the key bureaus, councils, and agencies in the community set up to deal with people in crisis (whether financial, legal, medical, etc.)?
4. What kind of problems or needs cause the greatest amount of difficulty and concern for the residents within the community?
5. What community-based organizations exist that target the special needs of some particular population group struggling with some particular problem or issue (e.g., Alcoholics Anonymous, volunteer groups, D.A.R.E., etc.)?
6. What kinds of networks exist that enable or help the community and its people helping agencies coordinate its helping activities?
7. What are the ten most used public agencies dealing with residents with special needs and problems? What is the phone number and addresses of these agencies, and who among them are in charge?
8. What role have the churches taken in dealing with some of the pressing concerns of the community or its parishes? What churches or church leaders have special programs designed to meet the needs of those who are most vulnerable in the community?
9. What kinds of money, scholarships, grants, fellowships, endowments, or allocations are available locally, statewide, or nationally to remedy some of the community's problems?
10. Who is in charge of administering or allocating these resources and funds?

XII. What Is the Status of Minority Groups within the Community?

1. What racial, ethnic, national, and cultural groups or families are represented in the community?
2. What section(s) of the community do these groups currently reside?
3. What has been the past legacy or relationship that the community has had with minority groups in the past? What is the history of the community in regard to its care for minority groups?

Source: *Planting Churches among the City's Poor, Volume 1*, pp. 405-417

4. What is the predominant perception of the various minority groups towards their community and their life within it?
5. Is there ill-will between the majority culture and minorities within the community? If so, how has this ill-will been expressed?
6. What evidences of injustice, segregation, mistreatment, and/or discrimination can be found in the life of the community (e.g., in the schools, hospitals, places of entertainment, etc.)?
7. Do equal opportunities exist for housing, police protection, employment, and leadership within community posts?
8. What churches, organizations, or community centers do minorities within the community frequent and congregate?
9. How does the media depict the minority population within the community?

XIII. What Is the Religious Character and Expression within the Community?

1. How does the community envision its own religious identity?
2. What are the major religious affiliations within the community (e.g., Christian, Judaism, Islam, Buddhism, Taoism, etc.)? How many belong to each affiliation, how long has the tradition been present within the community, and who are the respective leaders of each tradition within the community?
3. What percentage of the community attends some type of religious event regularly on daily, weekly, monthly, or annually?
4. What is the predominant religious group in the community?
5. What kind and number of Christian churches (Catholic, Protestant, or Orthodox) exist in the area?
6. How much does cultic or sectarian behavior influence the residents of the community (i.e., Jehovah's Witnesses, Mormons, Black Muslims, etc.)?
7. How does the community celebrate major religious holidays/events/festivals?
8. Who are the key religious figures in the community? What is the nature of the relationship and dialogue among them?
9. What kind of missionizing and religious outreach activities are currently taking place within the community?
10. To what degree is religious life and affiliation associated with cultural, racial, economic, or lifestyle lines of the greater secular community?

Source:
Planting Churches among the City's Poor, Volume 1, pp. 405-417

11. What evidence exists to affirm or deny the community's spiritual readiness and openness to the gospel?
12. What opportunities exist for Christian care-givers to cooperate in their outreach and people-helping ministries within the community?
13. How many Christian organizations are based and operate out of the community? What are they and what needs or problems do they seek to address? Who are the leaders of these various organizations?

XIV. What Is the Community's Awareness of the Larger Community of Which it Is a Part?

1. To what degree are the citizens aware or interested and informed of local, state, national or international events?
2. What issues of neighboring communities are of central importance for the residence of your community?
3. Comparatively speaking, what percentage of the city's overall resources and goods are used by the residents within the community?
4. What is the city's overall perception of the life and potential of the community?
5. What kind of partnerships and alliances exist between political and financial leaders of this community and leaders of other communities citywide?
6. What issues are of special weight or importance in the community's involvement in city, state, and national issues?
7. How have city policies directly influenced or shaped the ongoing life of the community in the last few years?
8. Who are the key liaisons or representatives of local or state governments assigned to the community? Where are city and state offices located within the community?
9. What organizations and institutions promote involvement in citizenship issues, political action, and education about national and world affairs?
10. What interest groups from outside the community have fought for the allegiance of the residents within the community? How have these interest groups been able to shape and influence community opinion?

Source: *Planting Churches among the City's Poor, Volume 1*, pp. 405-417

11. What percentage of residents have been actively involved in civic affairs that are of importance to the overall community and city's welfare? What is the nature of their involvement and participation?
12. How often do the leaders within the community interact with other community leaders regarding their needs, perceptions' and concerns?

XV. Who Is Meeting the Existing Needs of the Community?

1. What are the key organizations and institutions at work in the community overall in meeting the community's most critical needs?
2. In what ways are these groups currently cooperating to meet its needs?
3. What is the current role of churches in this effort?
4. Who are the key pastors, and what is their opinion as to the need for the church to be involved in community advancement?

XVI. What Is Our Christian Responsibility to Our Community?

1. In light of the available information and resources at our disposal, what is our obligation to this community?
2. What specific community ministry should our organization, congregation, or alliance explore further and undertake for the community in the immediate future?

Source: *Ripe for Harvest,* pp. 85-87

Church Planting Models

Rev. Dr. Don L. Davis

The following models represent a spectrum of models which have been associated with evangelical church planting. Questions are designed to help us explore the various options available to the cross-cultural urban church planter in establishing congregations among the poor. Our dialogue today hopefully will isolate some of the critical issues necessary for a church plant team to think through in order to make its selection as to what particular kind of church they ought to plant, given the culture, population, and other factors encountered in its particular mission field.

1. What is the definition of the phrase "church planting models"? Why might it be important to consider various options in planting a church among the poor in the city?

2. How would you characterize the various models (or other) which have been allowed or employed in traditional church planting? What would you consider to be its strengths and/or weaknesses, and should we use any or them in our planting of churches among the poor in the city?

   a. Founding Pastor Model – a leader moves into a community with a commitment to lead and shepherd the church that is planted.

   b. Church Split Model?! – a new church is formed due to fundamental disagreement over some issue of morality, Bible interpretation, or schism.

   c. Nucleus Model – (sometimes referred to as the "colonization" model). This model involves a central assembly commissioning a smaller nucleus from its group (usually with leadership and members already organized) to leave the larger assembly and relocate into an unreached community as a kind of ready-made nucleus of the church which is to be formed.

   d. Beachhead or Mother Church Model – a strong, central congregation determines to become a kind of sending center and nurturing headquarters for new churches planted through its oversight and auspices, in the immediate area and/or beyond.

Source: *Ripe for Harvest,* pp. 85-87

e. Cell Church Model – once centralized assembly which considers the heart of its life and ministry to occur in the cells which are connected structurally and pastorally to the central congregation; their participation together constitutes the church.

f. Home Church Model – a church, which although similar to a cell church model, is intentionally planted with greater attention given to the authority and autonomy of the gathering of Christians who meet regularly in their respective homes.

g. Missionary Model – a church where a cross-cultural church planter seeks to plant a church among an unreached people with an intent from the beginning to help the church to be self-propagating, self-governing, and self-supporting.

3. Instead of models language, World Impact recognizes three distinct "expressions" of church planting, out of which various models can be considered and employed.

The Small Church Expression (or "house church," 20-50 people). The small (or house) church can be understood as a *small store in a shopping mall.* It needs the connections to other small churches to both survive and thrive. Small churches are able to meet virtually anywhere and can operate with a tiny footprint with little to no financial burdens. They can focus on a specific block, housing development, or network of families. This expressions allows for a strong discipleship focus of indigenous leadership development can take place in this smaller connected group.

The Community Church Expression (60-150 people)
The community church is the most common expression of church, numerically speaking, in the world today. This expression can be understood as a *grocery or convenience store in a neighborhood or community.* This expression focuses on a particular geographic identity and proximity, highlighting both the, affinity, connection, and unique context of the congregation and the surrounding community. It is developed around a deep calling and connection to a particular neighborhood, and typically requires a semi-stable place to meet (e.g., a park, community center, or school). Partnership with other community churches is important.

The Mother Church Expression (200+ people)
The mother church (or "hub church") represents a larger assembly of believers, and can be understood as *a Walmart Superstore or Super*

Context
Values/Vision
Prepare
Launch
Assemble
Nurture
Transition
Schedule/Charter

Source:
Ripe for Harvest,
pp. 85-87

Target, a store which houses a number of select entities that supply its patrons with many choices and opportunities. This kind of church, which has both the economic and spiritual resources for multiplication, can leverage its resources and capabilities to become both a sending/empowering church which reproduces itself many times over. Ideally, a mother or hub church is a congregation that is led by clear missional intents that allow it to leverages its capabilities and gifts to become a center of compassion, mercy, and justice ministries. It can also come to serve as the nurturing headquarters for church planters and ministry starters, and can easily operate as an incubator of other effective ministries among the unreached urban poor. Such an expression usually is more rooted in a particular built-to-suit facility that allows it to leverage these kinds of capabilities.

4. What are the critical issues (e.g., culture, the tradition of the church planters, and contextualization) which ought to be factored most into selecting the appropriate model or expression for use in planting a church cross-culturally in the city?

5. Of all the things which a church planter may be aware of, what do you believe is the central element he or she must understand in order to choose the "right" option for them?

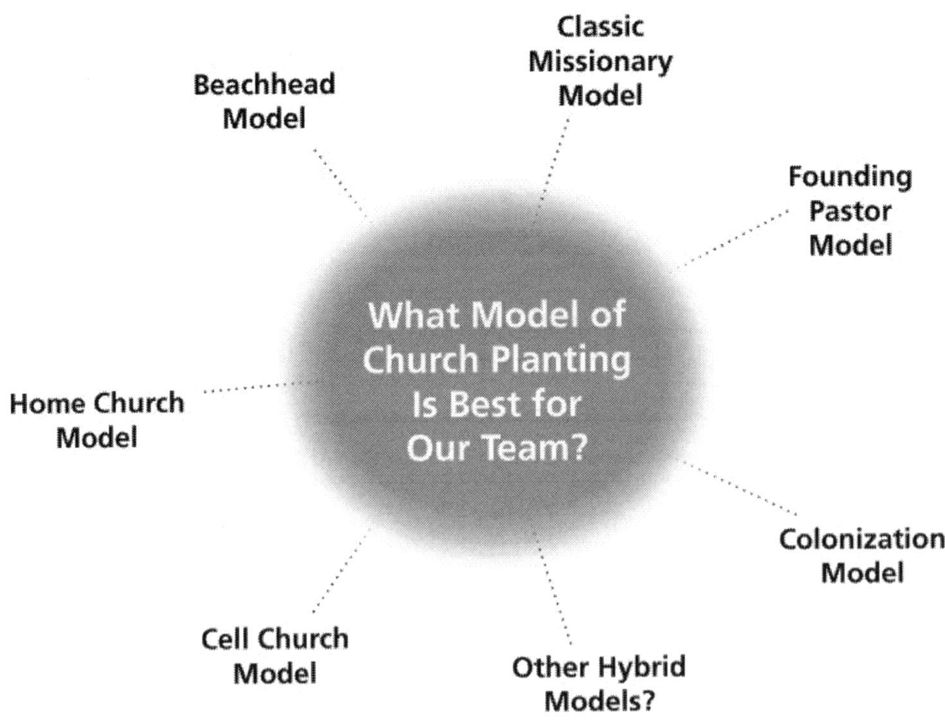

Context
Values/Vision
Prepare
Launch
Assemble
Nurture
Transition
Schedule/Charter

Source: *Planting Churches among the City's Poor, Volume 2,* pp. 332-333

Membership Commissioning Service

Anyname Fellowship Church

The Urban Ministry Institute

[Ask those individuals who intend to join our church family to stand.]

Commissioner

In the presence of the Lord God, the God and Father of our Lord Jesus, and in the company of the saints of this assembly, we gather to acknowledge you all together as members of our fellowship, the Anyname Fellowship Church family. On your profession of faith in Christ Jesus as your personal Lord and Savior, and by virtue of our knowledge of your personal walk with him and commitment to this church, we welcome you into our family upon your answer of the following questions.

As a member of Anyname, will you strive through the Spirit's leading to grow in grace and in the knowledge of Jesus Christ?

[Members say, "I will."]

Will you gather regularly and faithfully with the other members of our church family, and actively participate in our body life, fellowship, and service together?

[Members say, "I will."]

Will you allow the Lord to faithfully use your life and gifts to build up the members of this body, and to whomsoever the Lord will lead, as he gives you the strength and opportunity?

[Members say, "I will."]

Will you generously support the church's life and ministry together by giving your time, money, and other resources for its growth and mission in the world?

[Members say, "I will."]

Will you reach out and share the good news of the gospel with your unsaved friends, relatives, neighbors, and associates to become Christ's disciples, and members of his family?

[Members say, "I will."]

Source: *Planting Churches among the City's Poor, Volume 2,* pp. 332-333

Will you seek to build up the members of this body, as well as support and be responsive to the church's elected and appointed leaders?

[Members say, "I will."]

In light of your profession of faith and public commitment in the presence of the Lord and this assembly, we welcome you into our family, to share in all the privileges, responsibilities, and challenges that we share as Christ's body together.

Let us pray.

[Commissioner prays to the Lord.]

Let's greet together the new members of our Anyname church family!

Church Planting Movements

Source:
Ripe for Harvest,
pp. 23-28

Introduction
Sacred Roots, Church Planting, and the Great Tradition

Sacred Roots, Church Planting, and the Great Tradition

This essay was previously entitled "Going Forward by Looking Back: Toward an Evangelical Retrieval of the Great Tradition" by Don L. Davis (Wichita: TUMI Press, 2008). We are inserting it here as a fine introduction to this guidebook, since it concisely explains the fundamental importance of rediscovering the roots of our faith in our theology, worship, discipleship, and mission. We are convinced that we must place our activity of evangelism, discipleship, church planting, and mission in the context of what the Church has done and believed – always, everywhere, and by all of us. As church planters we must rediscover the apostolic faith, contextualize it among particular people groups, and then train them to express culturally that faith in a way that defends, extends, and embodies the one, true faith which the Church has always held. For those of us who long to see the Good News come alive in places where Jesus has never been known (i.e., the world's urban poor), this message is essential for us to remember – and to relearn. As we progress through the stages of church planting among the city's poor, we must stay aware of these insights, and strive to implement them in every facet of our outreach and empowerment.

Rediscovering the "Great Tradition"

In a wonderful little book, Ola Tjorhom,[1] describes the Great Tradition of the Church (sometimes called the "classical Christian tradition") as "living, organic, and dynamic."[2] The Great Tradition represents that evangelical, apostolic, and catholic core of Christian faith and practice which came largely to fruition from 100-500 AD.[3] Its rich legacy and treasures represent the Church's confession of what the Church has always believed, the worship that the ancient, undivided Church celebrated and embodied, and the mission that it embraced and undertook.

While the Great Tradition can neither substitute for the Apostolic Tradition (i.e., the authoritative source of all Christian faith, the Scriptures), nor should it overshadow the living presence of Christ in the Church through the Holy Spirit, it is still authoritative and revitalizing for the people of God. It has and still can provide God's people through time with the substance of its confession and faith. The Great Tradition has been embraced and affirmed as authoritative by Catholic, Orthodox, Anglican, and Protestant theologians, those ancient and modern, as it has produced the seminal documents, doctrines, confessions, and practices of the Church (e.g., the canon of Scriptures, the doctrines of the Trinity, the deity of Christ, etc.).

Source: *Ripe for Harvest,* pp. 23-28

Many evangelical scholars today believe that the way forward for dynamic faith and spiritual renewal will entail looking back, not with sentimental longings for the "good old days" of a pristine, problem free early Church, or a naive and even futile attempt to ape their heroic journey of faith. Rather, with a critical eye to history, a devout spirit of respect for the ancient Church, and a deep commitment to Scripture, we ought to rediscover through the Great Tradition the seeds of a new, authentic, and empowered faith. We can be transformed as we retrieve and are informed by the core beliefs and practices of the Church before the horrible divisions and fragmentations of Church history.

Well, if we do believe we ought to at least look again at the early Church and its life, or better yet, are convinced even to retrieve the Great Tradition for the sake of renewal in the Church–what exactly are we hoping to get back? Are we to uncritically accept everything the ancient Church said and did as "gospel," to be truthful simply because it is closer to the amazing events of Jesus of Nazareth in the world? Is old "hip," in and of itself?

No. We neither accept all things uncritically, nor do we believe that old, in and of itself, is truly good. Truth for us is more than ideas or ancient claims; for us, truth was incarnated in the person of Jesus of Nazareth, and the Scriptures give authoritative and final claim to the meaning of his revelation and salvation in history. We cannot accept things simply because they are reported to have been done in the past, or begun in the past. Amazingly, the Great Tradition itself argued for us to be critical, to contend for the faith once delivered to the saints (Jude 3), to embrace and celebrate the tradition received from the Apostles, rooted and interpreted by the Holy Scriptures themselves, and expressed in Christian confession and practice.

Core Dimensions of the Great Tradition

While Tjorhom offers his own list of ten elements of the theological content of the Great Tradition that he believes is worthy of reinterpretation and regard,[4] I believe there are seven dimensions that, from a biblical and spiritual vantage point, can enable us to understand what the early Church believed, how they worshiped and lived, and the ways they defended their living faith in Jesus Christ. Through their allegiance to the documents, confessions, and practices of this period, the ancient Church bore witness to God's salvation promise in the midst of a pagan and crooked generation. The core of our current faith and practice was developed in this era, and deserves a second (and twenty-second) look.

Adapting, redacting, and extending Tjorhom's notions of the Great Tradition, I list here what I take to be, as a start, a simple listing of the

Source: *Ripe for Harvest*, pp. 23-28

critical dimensions that deserve our undivided attention and wholehearted retrieval.

The Apostolic Tradition. The Great Tradition is rooted in the Apostolic Tradition, i.e., the apostles' eyewitness testimony and firsthand experience of Jesus of Nazareth, their authoritative witness to his life and work recounted in the Holy Scriptures, the canon of our Bible today. The Church is apostolic, built on the foundation of the prophets and the apostles, with Christ himself being the Cornerstone. The Scriptures themselves represent the source of our interpretation about the Kingdom of God, that story of God's redemptive love embodied in the promise to Abraham and the patriarchs, in the covenants and experience of Israel, and which culminates in the revelation of God in Christ Jesus, as predicted in the prophets and explicated in the apostolic testimony.

The Ecumenical Councils and Creeds, Especially the Nicene Creed. The Great Tradition declares the truth and sets the bounds of the historic orthodox faith as defined and asserted in the ecumenical creeds of the ancient and undivided Church, with special focus on the Nicene Creed. Their declarations were taken to be an accurate interpretation and commentary on the teachings of the Apostles set in Scripture. While not the source of the Faith itself, the confession of the ecumenical councils and creeds represents the substance of its teachings,[5] especially those before the fifth century (where virtually all of the elemental doctrines concerning God, Christ, and salvation were articulated and embraced).[6]

The Ancient Rule of Faith. The Great Tradition embraced the substance of this core Christian faith in a rule, i.e., an ancient standard rule of faith, that was considered to be the yardstick by which claims and propositions regarding the interpretation of the biblical faith were to be assessed. This rule, when applied reverently and rigorously, can clearly allow us to define the core Christian confession of the ancient and undivided Church expressed clearly in that instruction and adage of Vincent of Lerins: "that which has always been believed, everywhere, and by all."[7]

The *Christus Victor* Worldview. The Great Tradition celebrates and affirms Jesus of Nazareth as the Christ, the promised Messiah of the Hebrew Scriptures, the risen and exalted Lord, and Head of the Church. In Jesus of Nazareth alone, God has reasserted his reign over the universe, having destroyed death in his dying, conquering God's enemies through his incarnation, death, resurrection, and ascension, and ransoming humanity from its penalty due to its transgression of the Law. Now resurrected from the dead, ascended and exalted at the right hand of God, he has sent the Holy Spirit into the world to empower the Church in its life and witness. The Church is to be considered the

Source:
Ripe for Harvest,
pp. 23-28

people of the victory of Christ. At his return, he will consummate his work as Lord. This worldview was expressed in the ancient Church's confession, preaching, worship, and witness. Today, through its liturgy and practice of the Church Year, the Church acknowledges, celebrates, embodies, and proclaims this victory of Christ: the destruction of sin and evil and the restoration of all creation.

The Centrality of the Church. The Great Tradition confidently confessed the Church as the people of God. The faithful assembly of believers, under the authority of the Shepherd Christ Jesus, is now the locus and agent of the Kingdom of God on earth. In its worship, fellowship, teaching, service, and witness, Christ continues to live and move. The Great Tradition insists that the Church, under the authority of its undershepherds and the entirety of the priesthood of believers, is visibly the dwelling of God in the Spirit in the world today. With Christ himself being the Chief Cornerstone, the Church is the family of God, the body of Christ, and the temple of the Holy Spirit. All believers, living, dead, and yet unborn – make up the one, holy, catholic (universal), and apostolic community. Gathering together regularly in believing assembly, members of the Church meet locally to worship God through Word and sacrament, and to bear witness in its good works and proclamation of the Gospel. Incorporating new believers into the Church through baptism, the Church embodies the life of the Kingdom in its fellowship, and demonstrates in word and deed the reality of the Kingdom of God through its life together and service to the world.

The Unity of the Faith. The Great Tradition affirms unequivocally the catholicity of the Church of Jesus Christ, in that it is concerned with keeping communion and continuity with the worship and theology of the Church throughout the ages (Church universal). Since there has been and can only be one hope, calling, and faith, the Great Tradition fought and strove for oneness in word, in doctrine, in worship, in charity.

The Evangelical Mandate of the Risen Christ. The Great Tradition affirms the apostolic mandate to make known to the nations the victory of God in Jesus Christ, proclaiming salvation by grace through faith in his name, and inviting all peoples to repentance and faith to enter into the Kingdom of God. Through acts of justice and righteousness, the Church displays the life of the Kingdom in the world today, and through its preaching and life together provides a witness and sign of the Kingdom present in and for the world (*sacramentum mundi*), and as the pillar and ground of the truth. As evidence of the Kingdom of God and custodians of the Word of God, the Church is charged to define clearly and defend the faith once for all delivered to the Church by the apostles.

Source:
Ripe for Harvest,
pp. 23-28

Conclusion: Finding Our Future by Looking Back

In a time where so many are confused by the noisy chaos of so many claiming to speak for God, it is high time for us to rediscover the roots of our faith, to go back to the beginning of Christian confession and practice, and see, if in fact, we can recover our identity in the stream of Christ worship and discipleship that changed the world. In my judgment, this can be done through a critical, evangelical appropriation of the Great Tradition, that core belief and practice which is the source of all our traditions, whether Catholic, Orthodox, Anglican, or Protestant.

Of course, specific traditions will continue to seek to express and live out their commitment to the Authoritative Tradition (i.e., the Scriptures) and Great Tradition through their worship, teaching, and service. Our diverse Christian traditions (little "t"), when they are rooted in and expressive of the teaching of Scripture and led by the Holy Spirit, will continue to make the Gospel clear within new cultures or sub-cultures, speaking and modeling the hope of Christ into new situations shaped by their own set of questions posed in light of their own unique circumstances. Our traditions are essentially movements of contextualization, that is, they are attempts to make plain within people groups the Authoritative Tradition in a way that faithfully and effectively leads them to faith in Jesus Christ.

We ought, therefore, to find ways to enrich our contemporary traditions by reconnecting and integrating our contemporary confessions and practices with the Great Tradition. Let us never forget that Christianity, at its core, is a faithful witness to God's saving acts in history. As such, we will always be a people who seek to find our futures by looking back through time at those moments of revelation and action where the Rule of God was made plain through the incarnation, passion, resurrection, ascension, and soon-coming of Christ. Let us then remember, celebrate, reenact, learn afresh, and passionately proclaim what believers have confessed since the morning of the empty tomb–the saving story of God's promise in Jesus of Nazareth to redeem and save a people for his own.

Endnotes

1 Ola Tjorhom, *Visible Church–Visible Unity: Ecumenical Ecclesiology and "The Great Tradition of the Church."* Collegeville, Minnesota: Liturgical Press, 2004. Robert Webber defined the Great Tradition in this way: "[It is] the broad outline of Christian belief and practice developed from the Scriptures between the time of Christ and the middle of the fifth century." Robert E. Webber, *The Majestic Tapestry*. Nashville: Thomas Nelson Publishers, 1986, p. 10.

2 Ibid., p. 35.

Source:
Ripe for Harvest,
pp. 23-28

3 The core of the Great Tradition concentrates on the formulations, confessions, and practices of the Church's first five centuries of life and work. Thomas Oden, in my judgment, rightly asserts that ". . . . most of what is enduringly valuable in contemporary biblical exegesis was discovered by the fifth century" (cf. Thomas C. Oden, *The Word of Life*. San Francisco: HarperSanFrancisco, 1989, p. xi.).

4 Ibid., pp. 27-29. Tjorhom's ten elements are argued in the context of his work where he also argues for the structural elements and the ecumenical implications of retrieving the Great Tradition. I wholeheartedly agree with the general thrust of his argument, which, like my own belief, makes the claim that an interest in and study of the Great Tradition can renew and enrich the contemporary Church in its worship, service, and mission.

5 I am indebted to the late Dr. Robert E. Webber for this helpful distinction between the source and the substance of Christian faith and interpretation.

6 While the seven ecumenical Councils (along with others) are affirmed by both Catholic and Orthodox communions as binding, it is the first four Councils that are to be considered the critical, most essential confessions of the ancient, undivided Church. I and others argue for this largely because the first four articulate and settle once and for all what is to be considered our orthodox faith on the doctrines of the Trinity and the Incarnation (cf. Philip Schaff, *The Creeds of Christendom*, v. 1. Grand Rapids: Baker Book House, 1996, p. 44). Similarly, even the magisterial Reformers embraced the teaching of the Great Tradition, and held its most significant confessions as authoritative. Correspondingly, Calvin could argue in his own theological interpretations that "Thus councils would come to have the majesty that is their due; yet in the meantime Scripture would stand out in the higher place, with everything subject to its standard. In this way, we willingly embrace and reverence as holy the early councils, such as those of Nicea, Constantinople, the first of Ephesus I, Chalcedon, and the like, which were concerned with refuting errors – in so far as they relate to the teachings of faith. For they contain nothing but the pure and genuine exposition of Scripture, which the holy Fathers applied with spiritual prudence to crush the enemies of religion who had then arisen" (cf. John Calvin, *Institutes of the Christian Religion*, IV, ix. 8. John T. McNeill, ed. Ford Lewis Battles, trans. Philadelphia: Westminster Press, 1960, pp. 1171-72).

7 This rule, which has won well-deserved favor down through the years as a sound theological yardstick for authentic Christian truth, weaves three cords of critical assessment to determine what may be counted as orthodox or not in the Church's teaching. St. Vincent of Lerins, a theological commentator who died before 450 AD, authored what has come to be called the "Vincentian canon, a three-fold test of catholicity: *quod ubique, quod semper, quod ab omnibus creditum est* (what has been believed everywhere, always and by all). By this three-fold test of ecumenicity, antiquity, and consent, the church may discern between true and false traditions." (cf. Thomas C. Oden, *Classical Pastoral Care*, vol. 4. Grand Rapids: Baker Books, 1987, p. 243).

The Nature of Dynamic Church Planting Movements

Defining the Elements of Effective Church Planting Movements

Rev. Dr. Don L. Davis

<table>
<tr><th colspan="7">A Missional Appraisal of Dynamic Church Planting Movements</th></tr>
<tr><th colspan="2">Elements</th><th>Shared Spirituality</th><th>People Group Identity</th><th>Dynamic Standardization</th><th>Level of Fruitfulness</th></tr>
<tr><td colspan="2">Term</td><td>Spiritual Formation</td><td>Contextualization</td><td>Multiplication</td><td rowspan="4"></td></tr>
<tr><td colspan="2">Definition</td><td>Possessing a common spiritual identity in a church body that expresses the Great Tradition</td><td>Affirming our freedom in Christ to embody the faith within ethnicity and culture</td><td>Rapidly reproducing healthy churches of a kind through shared protocols and resources</td></tr>
<tr><td colspan="2">Explanation</td><td>Presumes a valid, distinctive apostolic spiritual identity embodied in a church body (why and what)</td><td>Conditions how that identity is understood, practiced (where and with whom)</td><td>Determines how that identity is formed, nourished, and multiplied (how)</td></tr>
<tr><td colspan="2">Burden</td><td>To express a common spiritual vision and discipline in shared practice</td><td>To contextualize within a culture or people group</td><td>To organize and coordinate resources for the common good</td></tr>
<tr><td rowspan="4">Alternative Approaches in Church Planting</td><td>Model 1</td><td>Cultivated identity built on spirituality and practice</td><td>Full attention to culture and ethnicity</td><td>Integrated structures and common protocols</td><td>Most Effective</td></tr>
<tr><td>Model 2</td><td>Shared elements of spirituality and practice</td><td>More attention to culture and ethnicity</td><td>Voluntary structures and optional protocols</td><td>More Effective</td></tr>
<tr><td>Model 3</td><td>Divergent, dissimilar spirituality and practice</td><td>Some attention to culture and ethnicity</td><td>Iconoclastic structures and divergent protocols</td><td>Less Effective</td></tr>
<tr><td>Model 4</td><td>Fragmented approaches to spirituality and practice</td><td>No attention to culture and ethnicity</td><td>Arbitrary structures and random protocols</td><td>Least Effective</td></tr>
</table>

Source: *Planting Churches among the City's Poor, Volume 2,* p. 23

Creating Coherent Urban Church Planting Movements

Discerning the Elements of Authentic Urban Christian Community

Rev. Dr. Don L. Davis

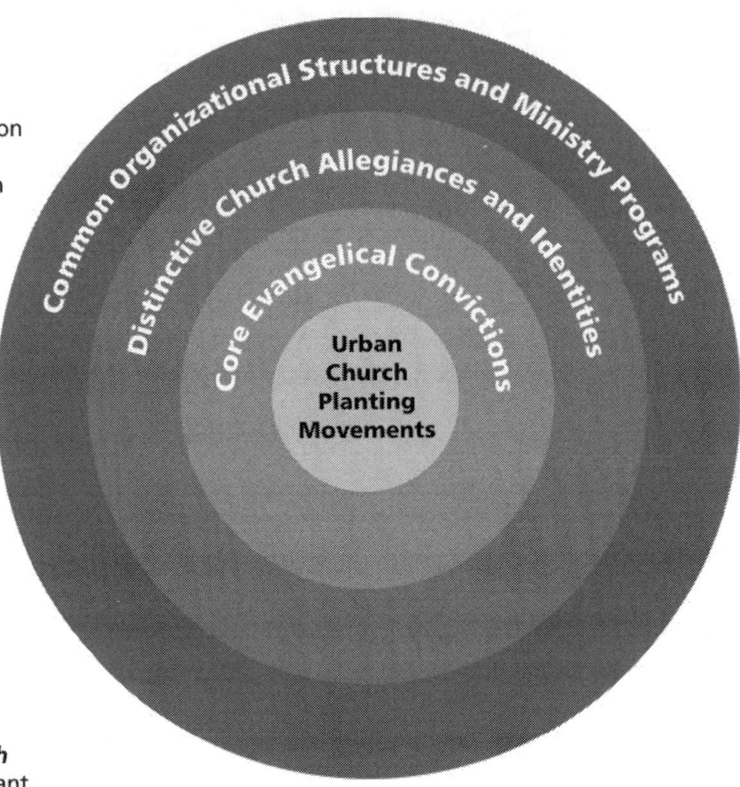

Core Evangelical Convictions

This circle represents ***its most fundamental convictions and commitments***, its Affirmation of Faith, its commitment to the Gospel and those truths contained in the early Christian creeds (i.e., The Nicene Creed). These convictions are anchored in its confidence in the Word of God, and represent our unequivocal commitment to historic orthodoxy.

As members of the one, holy, apostolic, and catholic (universal) body of Christ, movements must be **ready and willing to die for their core evangelical convictions**. These convictions serve as the connection of the movements to the historic Christian faith, and as such, can never be compromised or altered.

Distinctive Church Allegiances and Identities

This circle represents their distinctive ***church allegiances and identities***. Urban church plant movements will coalesce around their own distinctive traditions, overseen by leaders who provide those movements with vision, instruction, and direction as they move forward together to represent Christ and his Kingdom in the inner city.

Specific traditions seek to express and live out this faithfulness to the Authoritative and Great Traditions through their worship, teaching, and service. They seek to make the Gospel clear within new cultures or sub-cultures, speaking and modeling the hope of Christ into new situations shaped by their own set of questions posed in light of their own unique circumstances. These movements, therefore, seek to contextualize the Authoritative Tradition in a way that faithfully and effectively leads new groups of people to faith in Jesus Christ, and incorporates those who believe into the community of faith that obeys his teachings and gives witness of him to others.

Urban church plant movements must be **ready and willing to articulate and defend their unique distinctives** as God's kingdom community in the city.

Common Organizational Structure and Ministry Programs

This circle represents the ways in which coherent urban church plant movements express their convictions and identity ***through their own distinct organizational structures and ministry programs***. These structures and programs are designed and executed through their own specific strategies, policies, decisions, and procedures. The structures and programs represent their self-chosen methods of fleshing out their understanding of the faith as it pertains to their community purpose and mission. These are subject to change under their own legitimate processes as they apply accumulated wisdom in *how best* to accomplish their purposes in the city.

As a communities of faith in Christ, urban church movements must be encouraged to **dialogue about their structures and ministry programs** in order to discover the best possible means to contextualize the Gospel and advance the Kingdom of God among their neighbors.

Source: *Planting Churches among the City's Poor, Volume 2*, p. 25

The Threefold Cord of Urban Cross-Cultural Church Planting Movements

Rev. Dr. Don L. Davis

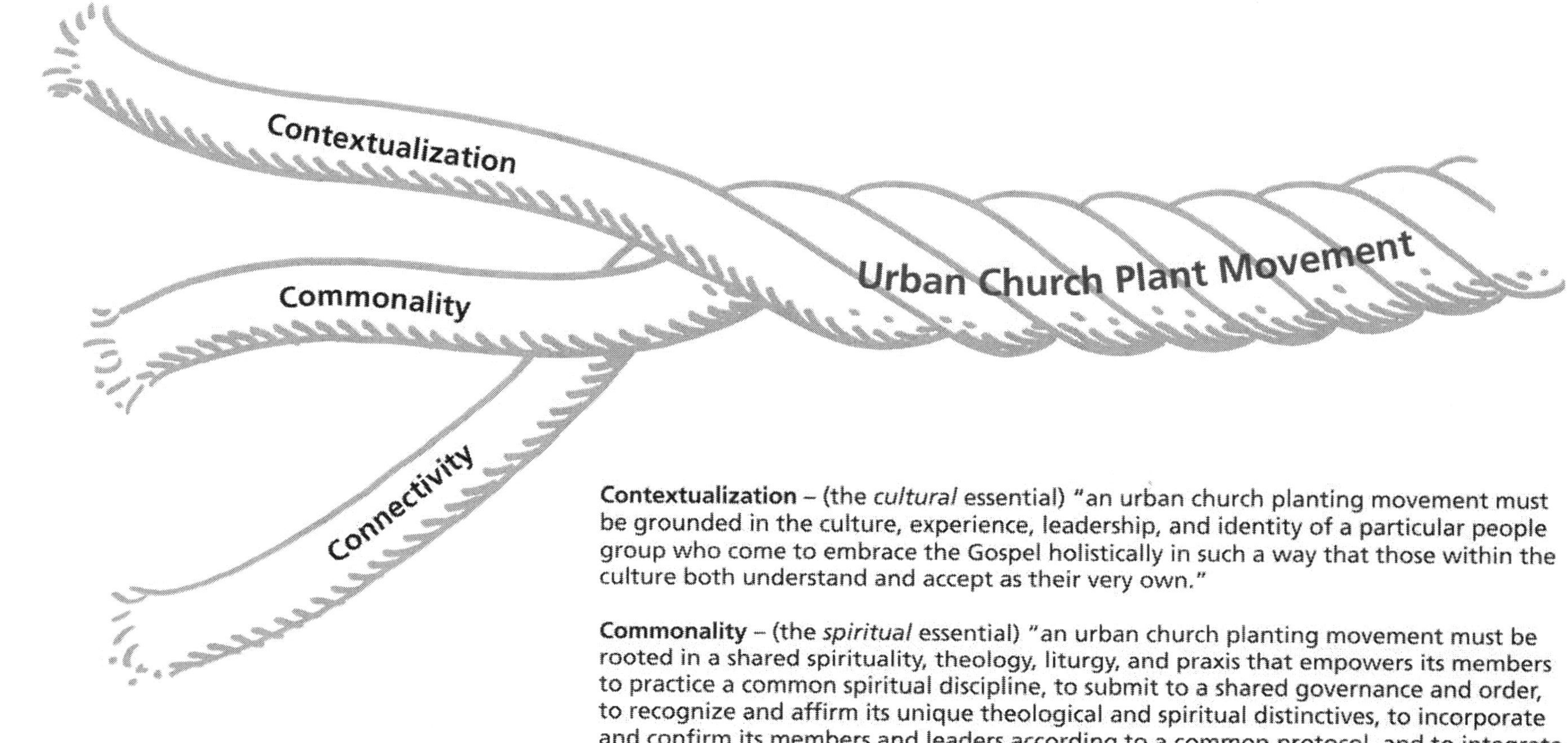

Ecc. 4.12 (ESV) - *And though a man might prevail against one who is alone, two will withstand him – a threefold cord is not quickly broken.*

Contextualization – (the *cultural* essential) "an urban church planting movement must be grounded in the culture, experience, leadership, and identity of a particular people group who come to embrace the Gospel holistically in such a way that those within the culture both understand and accept as their very own."

Commonality – (the *spiritual* essential) "an urban church planting movement must be rooted in a shared spirituality, theology, liturgy, and praxis that empowers its members to practice a common spiritual discipline, to submit to a shared governance and order, to recognize and affirm its unique theological and spiritual distinctives, to incorporate and confirm its members and leaders according to a common protocol, and to integrate the efforts of its congregations together into a coherent, unified movement."

Connectivity – (the *structural* essential) "an urban church planting movement must connect its leaders, members, and congregations through integrated structures that enable its congregations and leaders to gather regularly for convocation and fellowship, that combine resources and funds for cooperation and mutual support, and that provide oversight that protects and equips the members of the movement for dynamic reproduction."

Source: *Planting Churches among the City's Poor, Volume 2*, p. 270

A Model of an Urban Church Association

Rev. Dr. Don L. Davis

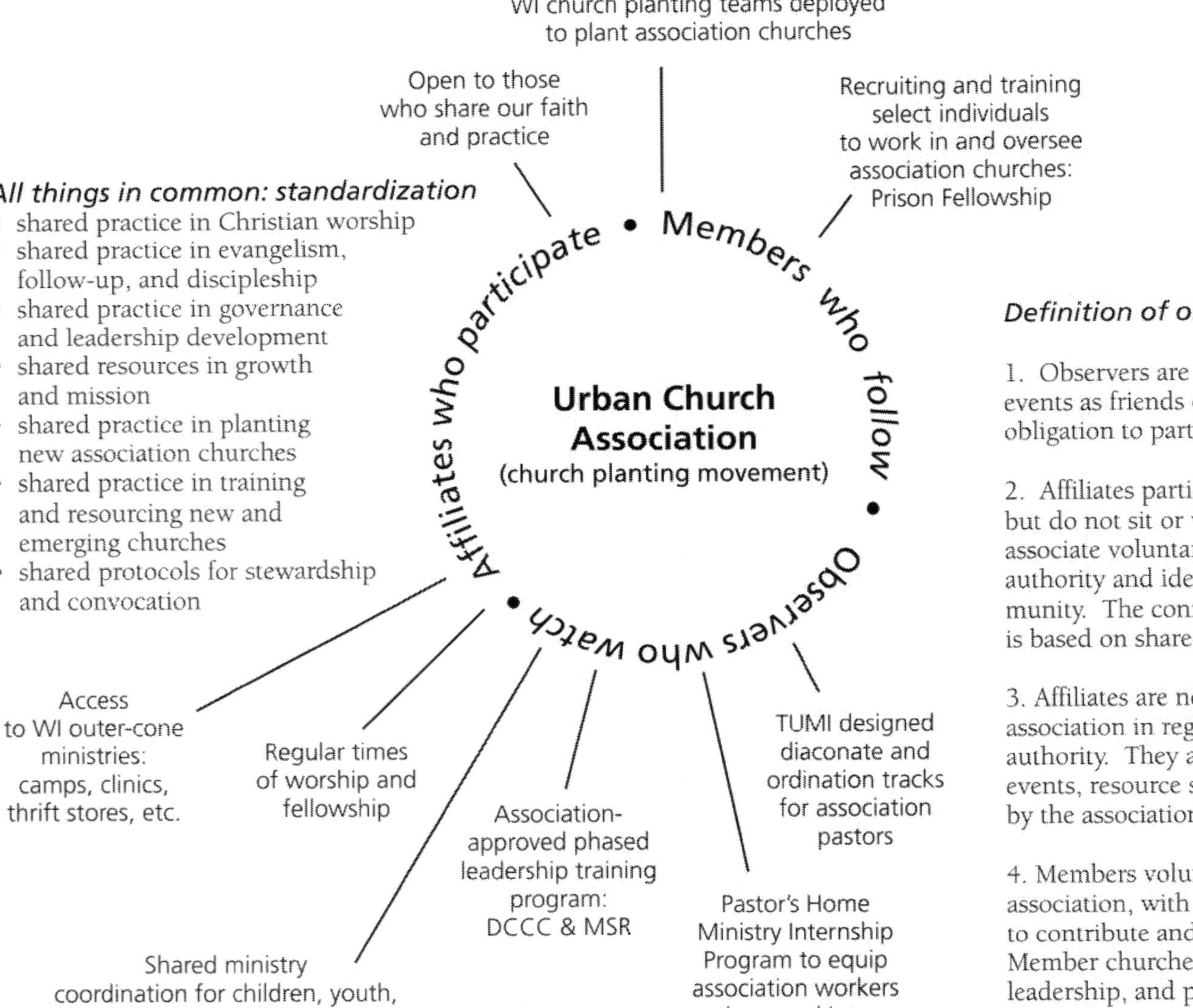

All things in common: standardization

- shared practice in Christian worship
- shared practice in evangelism, follow-up, and discipleship
- shared practice in governance and leadership development
- shared resources in growth and mission
- shared practice in planting new association churches
- shared practice in training and resourcing new and emerging churches
- shared protocols for stewardship and convocation

Affiliates – those leaders and congregations who participate in association events and resources but retain their own autonomy and identity within another church community.

Members – those leaders and congregations who voluntarily submit to the authority and identity of the association for their growth and mission.

Definition of observers, affiliates, and members.

1. Observers are allowed to attend select association events as friends of the association, with no further obligation to participate in its activities or initiatives.

2. Affiliates participate in sponsored association events, but do not sit or vote on its councils of authority. They associate voluntarily, that is, they retain their own authority and identity within their own church community. The connection they share with the association is based on shared values, resources, and mission.

3. Affiliates are not subject to decisions made by the association in regards to its doctrine, mission, and authority. They are limited to participate in those events, resource sharing, and mission projects allowed by the association.

4. Members voluntarily submit to the authority of the association, with full rights and privileges thereof, to contribute and represent it according to its protocols. Member churches are able to vote, be nominated for leadership, and participate in all levels of association business and mission.

Source: *Planting Churches among the City's Poor, Volume 2*, p. 27

Church Planting Roles and Responsibilities

Source: *Planting Churches among the City's Poor, Volume 1,* p. 336

Responsibilities of a Church Plant Team Leader

World Impact

- To *faithfully intercede* for oneself, one's members and volunteers, the community, and the entire effort during the Charter period
- To *relate and communicate regularly* with the Multiple Team Leader (MTL) and his/her Director and/or church authority on the status of the plant
- To commence the *John Mark Curriculum* and its prescribed courses for Team Leader development
- To attend *World Impact's Urban Church Plant School* with core team members and the MTL to develop a Team Charter
- To oversee *the formation and implementation of the team's church planting strategy*
- To insure that each team member has received *adequate orientation and training* for his/her role
- To care for *the spiritual and emotional welfare of the team*, both as individuals, and as a whole
- To *lead team meetings, and its processes* of planning, preparing, evaluating, and making adjustments to the Charter
- To help team members *resolve interpersonal conflict*
- To *secure resources, personnel, and counseling* for the team's ongoing challenges and opportunities
- To set an *example of service and spirituality* for the team

Source: *Planting Churches among the City's Poor, Volume 1,* pp. 371-374

Forming the Church Plant Team and Understanding the Roles

Excerpted from *The Nehemiah Team Training Materials*

I. The Team (four types of members)

A. Core members (the primary job of the core member is church planting): four to six people

1. Meet for planning, outreach, and worship at least two weekday evenings and some weekend time

2. Stay in active service with the team for a minimum of two years

3. Called by God and willing to engage in cross-cultural evangelism

4. The team leader must be a core team member

B. Support team members

1. Stay in active service for a minimum of 3 months

2. Meet weekly with the team for planning and prayer

3. Give at least one weekday evening and/or some weekend time to serve church plant

C. Volunteers: Individuals or groups

1. Serve as needed on a project-by-project basis

2. Are invited to planning meetings and projects that pertain to them, but do not function as week-to-week team members

D. Indigenous leaders

1. The goal of all core team members, support team members and volunteers is replacement by indigenous leadership.

2. The team function moves from doing to equipping.

Source: *Planting Churches among the City's Poor, Volume 1*, pp. 371-374

3. As the church plant progresses, more and more of the team becomes people won to Christ during the church planting process.

    a. Avoid dependency.

    b. Think reproducibility.

II. Leadership of the Team

A. The leader of the church plant team is appointed by the leadership of the sending church.

1. He or she is co-leader with World Impact's staff member assigned to lead the team through the church planting process. Together they:

    a. Lead the team in prayer, strategy formulation, execution of plans, and evaluation of progress

    b. Train the team

    c. Regularly inform sending church and World Impact of progress and needs

2. Specific responsibilities of team leader:

    a. Facilitate meetings

    b. Make sure that there is excellent communication among the team

    c. Maintain excellent communication with leadership of sending church regarding progress and needs

    d. Meet regularly with World Impact coach (separate from the team)

    e. Provide pastoral care for team members

    f. Maintain team unity

    g. Provide leadership for the church that is planted (assume role as pastor) until replacement is trained

Source: *Planting Churches among the City's Poor, Volume 1,* pp. 371-374

B. Specific responsibilities of World Impact coach:

1. Train the team in principles of urban church planting

2. Provide practical ongoing guidance for how to accomplish each step of the church planting process

3. Meet regularly with team leader

4. Provide expert counsel to team in planning meetings

5. Help the team execute plans

6. Help the team evaluate programs and make adjustments

7. Help team utilize World Impact support ministries for enhancing their church planting efforts

C. The sending church is ultimately responsible for the spiritual accountability and oversight of their appointed leader and church plant members.

D. The core members, support members, volunteer members, and indigenous leaders will be expected to submit to the authority of the team leader and the World Impact coach.

III. Beginning Activities to Build Team Cohesion

A. Get to know each other.

1. Eat together.

2. Share testimonies.

3. Share individual visions.

4. Pray for each other.

5. Retreat together.

B. Work on forging a common vision and strategy for this project and training each team member to articulate it.

Source: *Planting Churches among the City's Poor, Volume 1,* pp. 371-374

C. Pray together for the target community.

1. Pray for the establishment of God's Church and Kingdom.

2. Pray against strongholds of evil.

D. Worship God corporately.

Source: *Planting Churches among the City's Poor, Volume 1*, p. 467

Key Roles of a Church Planting Team

World Impact

- Evangelist (good at developing relationships with new people to lead them to God)
- Worship leader
- Children's ministry leader
- Shepherd/care-giver (good at nurturing the believers)
- Organizer (organizes special projects and builds systems to turn vision into reality)
- Administrator (administrates systems to help team accomplish goals)
- Church Planter (roles that can't be delegated)
  - ~ Spiritual leadership and vision casting
  - ~ Team building and supervision
  - ~ Modeling pastoral care and evangelism
  - ~ Overall leadership of small group ministry

Source: *Planting Churches among the City's Poor, Volume 2,* p. 69

Responsibilities of a Coach (Multiple Team Leader)

- To *faithfully intercede* for each team and Team Leader during the oversight period.
- To *relate and communicate regularly* with each Team Leader and his/her Director and/or church authority as you provide strategic oversight for the duration of the Team's Charter.
- To commence the *John Mark Curriculum* and its prescribed courses for Multiple Team Leader development.
- To attend *World Impact's Urban Church Plant School* with the Team Leader and his/her core members, and work with the team as they develop their Charter.
- To enable Team Leaders and their teams *to implement a credible, contextualized PWR process* in their outreach.
- To help each team fulfill its Charter by *formally evaluating the team's progress at each prescribed evaluation date*, and any other time deemed necessary.
- To submit *responses to each Team's formal evaluation* to World Impact Director or church authority.
- To receive *regular input from each Team Leader*, and offer follow-up, input, and correction where it is needed or when the plan needs definition and clarity.
- To *renew or revise the Charter* when it expires, or recommend its discontinuation if circumstances warrant.

Equipping the Church Plant Team Member

Developing Workable Training Strategies

Rev. Dr. Don L. Davis

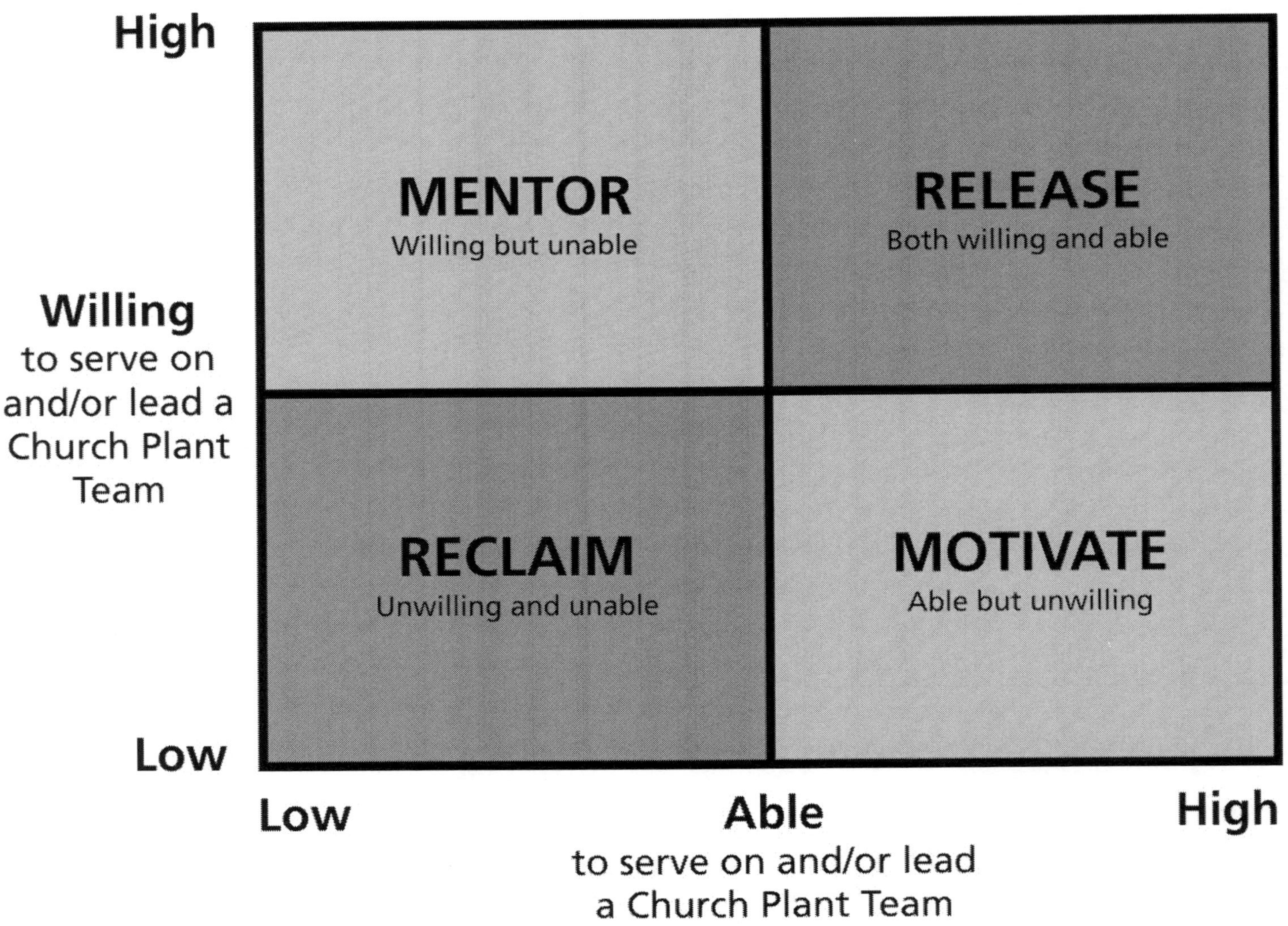

Willing to serve on and/or lead a Church Plant Team	**Able** to serve on and/or lead a Church Plant Team: **Low**	**Able** to serve on and/or lead a Church Plant Team: **High**
High	**MENTOR** Willing but unable	**RELEASE** Both willing and able
Low	**RECLAIM** Unwilling and unable	**MOTIVATE** Able but unwilling

Source: *Planting Churches among the City's Poor, Volume 2*, p. 78

Empowering Indigenous Leadership

Investment, Empowerment, and Assessment

How Leadership as Representation Provides Freedom to Innovate

Rev. Dr. Don L. Davis

Formal leadership selection	Evaluation by sending authority
Acknowledgment of personal call	Review of results in light of task
Determination of task and assignment	Faithfulness and loyalty assessed
Training in spiritual warfare	Overall evaluation of plan and strategy
Authorization to act defined and given	Critical evaluation of leadership performance
Necessary resources given and logistics planned	Formal determination of operation's "success"
Commissioning: deputization formally recognized	Reassignment in light of evaluation

Source: *Planting Churches among the City's Poor, Volume 2,* p. 138

Nurturing Authentic Christian Leadership

Rev. Dr. Don L. Davis

Cliff On-One-Side	Cliff On-the-Other-Side
Laying on hands too quickly	Always postponing delegation to indigenous
Ignoring culture in leadership training	Elevating culture above truth
Demoting doctrine and theology	Supposing doctrine and theology as only criteria
Highlighting skills and gifts above availability and character	Substituting availability and character for genuine giftedness
Emphasizing administrative abilities above spiritual dynamism	Ignoring administration's role in spiritual vitality and power
Equating readiness with Christian perfection	Ignoring the importance of biblical standards
Limiting candidacy for leadership based on gender and ethnicity	Setting quotas of leadership based on gender and ethnicity
Seeing everyone as a leader	Seeing virtually no one as worthy to lead

Source: *Planting Churches among the City's Poor, Volume 2,* p. 163

Source: *Planting Churches among the City's Poor, Volume 2,* pp. 119-125

Summary of the Capstone Curriculum

The Urban Ministry Institute

The Capstone Curriculum is a 16-module training program, taught at a seminary level, which we specifically designed to serve as the most essential knowledge and skill learning necessary for effective urban ministry. Each module (course) comes with a Mentor's Guide, a Student Workbook and two DVD's (four hours of video). Each module also has required supplemental textbooks.

An Overview of the Capstone Curriculum

The Capstone Curriculum is a 16-module training program, taught at a seminary level, which we specifically designed to serve as the most essential knowledge and skill learning necessary for effective urban ministry and church leadership. Although each module contains its own specific list of objectives to guide mentors and students through the material, below you will find our eight overall objectives we seek to implement across our Capstone Curriculum:

- To ground emerging urban leaders in the Gospel of Christ, enabling them to know the basics of conversion and their own calling to salvation and leadership
- To root our students in the indispensability of the Church to serve as both agent and locus of the Kingdom, and for them to serve the church practically and specifically in the local assembly
- To equip urban leaders with the necessary study skills to study, apply, teach, preach, and minister the Word of God in the urban context, applying their learning in the context of their own personal lives and church ministries
- To challenge urban leaders to regularly memorize select portions of Scripture, and develop the discipline of review to retain and utilize texts both devotionally and in ministry
- To establish urban leaders in a Christ-centered vision of Scripture, and equip them in a Nicene-based, biblical theology that is congruent with the historic orthodox faith of the Great Tradition
- To provide a biblical foundation for both understanding and practicing Christian leadership in the context of the Church, with a special emphasis and appreciation for spiritual formation in urban communities, especially among the poor

Source:
Planting Churches among the City's Poor, Volume 2,
pp. 119-125

- To train urban leaders to evangelize, disciple, plant, pastor, and minister within evangelical urban churches which will be spiritually vital, culturally conducive, and aggressively reproductive within the various people groups needing Christ in the city
- To encourage urban leaders to find practical, meaningful ways to promote justice and demonstrate mercy with the broken and needy in urban communities, and discover ways to display hospitality, generosity, and compassion in the places where they live and minister

Each module (course) comes with a Mentor's Guide, a Student Workbook and two DVD's (four hours of video). Each module also has required supplemental textbooks. This curriculum is designed to be used in a variety of formats, time frames, and venues. As a complete training curriculum, it may be accessed through The Urban Ministry Institute's Satellite Certificate program. Affectionately called "a seminary in a box," this curriculum will give you everything you need to equip yourself and your leaders for effective ministry in your church and community.

On our website, *www.tumi.org/Capstone*, you will find the following additional resources regarding Capstone:

- ***An Overview of the Capstone Curriculum with all of the Module Descriptions and Lesson Objectives***

  This is a very helpful document that will give you information on Capstone for your review. This document will help you get a thorough understanding of the overall schema of Capstone as well as each particular module's content and objectives. This is the document that our partners have used to determine their level of accreditation for our resource and their institution of higher education. This is a great resource for your mentors!

- ***Capstone Module Descriptions***

  This document has all 16 Capstone Module descriptions in one file. This document is a great tool to help you understand what each module is about in relatively few pages.

- ***The Capstone Curriculum at a Glance***

  Included in this packet as well, this two-page document provides an at-a-glance look at our entire Capstone Curriculum (including lesson titles), and also defines our terminology in this structure programming, along with breakdown of the modules and the outline of the lessons.

Source: *Planting Churches among the City's Poor, Volume 2,* pp. 119-125

- ***Capstone Module Sample***

  Are you interested in hearing actual module teaching? Feel free to preview one of the Capstone module's instruction to gain a better understanding of what we've included in each module. Listening to the teaching may convince you that our training may be appropriate and desirable for your church or ministry leadership training!

- ***Required Textbooks***

  Each Capstone module has assigned textbooks which are read and discussed through the course. We encourage students to read, reflect upon, and respond to these with their professors, mentors, and fellow learners. Because of the fluidity of the texts (i.e., books going out of print), the required textbook list will change and most likely will be different from what is listed in your Capstone Curriculum workbook. This is the OFFICIAL Capstone required textbook list.

- ***Module Information for each of the 16 Capstone Modules***

  Our site gives links to each Capstone Module's course information, along with its summary and description (included in this packet), and both its required and supplemental textbooks.

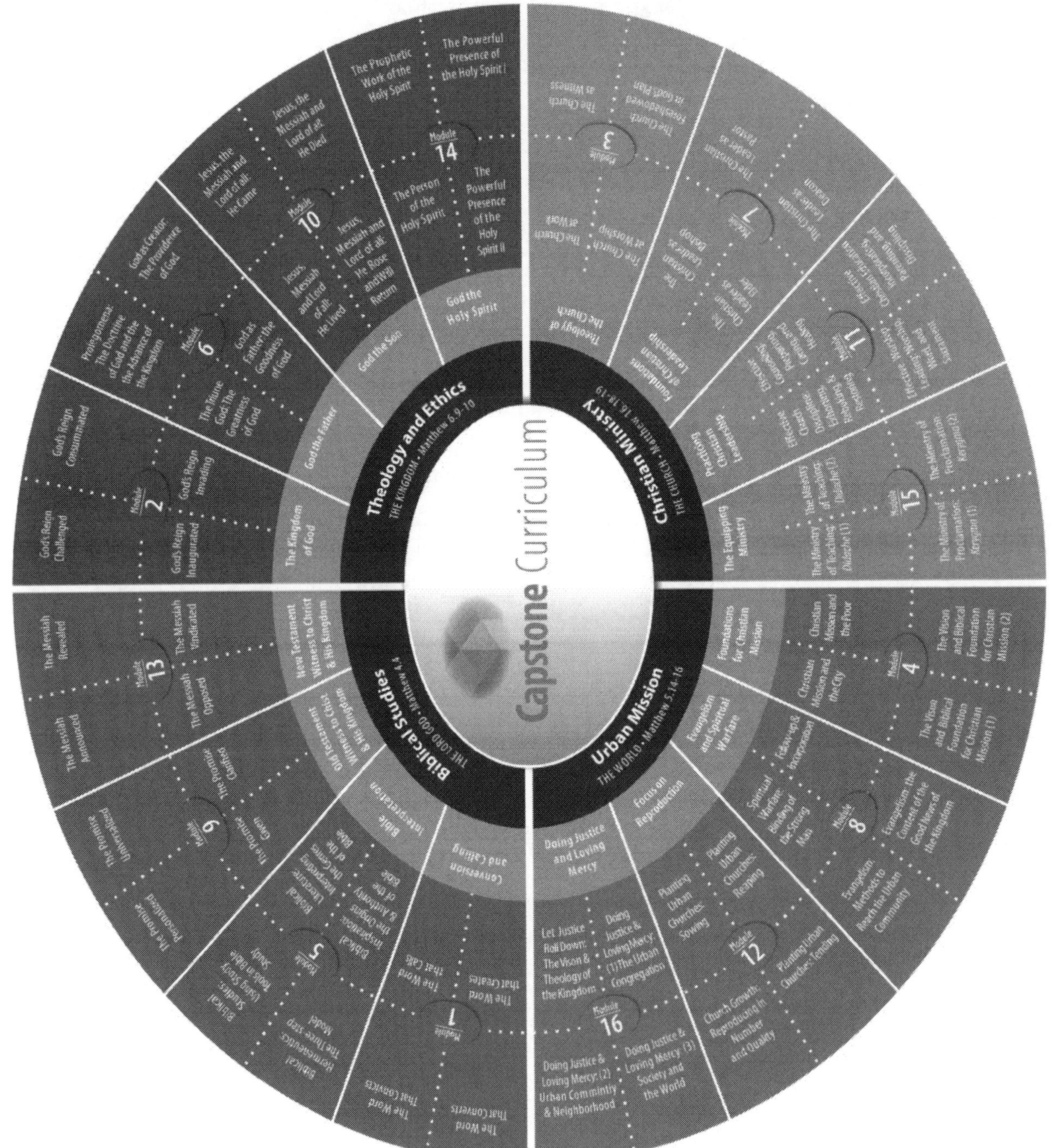

Source: *Planting Churches among the City's Poor, Volume 2*, pp. 119-125

The Capstone Curriculum Developing Urban Christian Leaders for the Church and the Kingdom – Matthew 21.42							
Biblical Studies *The Lord God • Matt. 4.4*		Theology and Ethics *The Kingdom • Matt. 6.9-10*		Christian Ministry *The Church • Matt. 16.18-19*		Urban Mission *The World • Matt. 5.14-16*	
1	Conversion and Calling	2	The Kingdom of God	3	Theology of the Church	4	Foundations for Christian Mission
5	Bible Interpretation	6	God the Father	7	Foundations of Christian Leadership	8	Evangelism and Spiritual Warfare
9	The Old Testament Witness to Christ and His Kingdom	10	God the Son	11	Practicing Christian Leadership	12	Focus on Reproduction
13	The New Testament Witness to Christ and His Kingdom	14	God the Holy Spirit	15	The Equipping Ministry	16	Doing Justice and Loving Mercy: Compassion Ministries

Terminology

The Capstone Curriculum

The entire four unit, sixteen subject teaching program designed to develop urban Christian leadership for the Church and the Kingdom

Department Area

Four subjects organized under the headings of either Biblical Studies, Theology and Ethics, Christian Ministry, or Urban Mission

Module

One subject in a unit

Lesson

An individual teaching presentation in a module

Segment

A twenty-five minute video teaching normally used in a lesson

A Capstone Module

- Each module is divided into four lessons
- Each module is designed to be taught in 12 classroom hours surpassing the well-accepted "CEU" (Continuing Education Unit) standards
- Each module features a Student Workbook, a Mentor's Guide, and two DVDs (4 hours of video)

Source: *Planting Churches among the City's Poor, Volume 2,* pp. 119-125

Source: *Planting Churches among the City's Poor, Volume 2,* pp. 119-125

Sample Lesson Outline (Three hour lesson)

Attendance and Quiz . . . . (20 minutes)
Mentor-led Contact section . . . . (10 minutes)
First Video Segment . . . . (25 minutes)
Student Question/Response . . . . (20 minutes)
Break . . . . (15 minutes)
Second Video Segment . . . . (25 minutes)
Student Question/Response . . . . (20 minutes)
Mentor-led Connection . . . . (45 minutes)

- Student Application and Implications Discussion
- Case Studies and Problems
- Assignments
- Ministry Projects
- Counseling and Prayer

The *Capstone Curriculum* is designed to be used in a variety of formats, time frames, and venues. As a complete training curriculum, it may be accessed through The Urban Ministry Institute's Certificate Program. As a modular program, the *Capstone Curriculum* may be taught as seminars, workshops, conferences, small groups, or various other applications.

The Capstone Curriculum Developing Urban Christian Leaders for the Church and the Kingdom – Matthew 21.42			
Biblical Studies *The Lord God • Matt. 4.4*	Theology and Ethics *The Kingdom • Matt. 6.9-10*	Christian Ministry *The Church • Matt. 16.18-19*	Urban Mission *The World • Matt. 5.14-16*
1 Conversion and Calling	2 The Kingdom of God	3 Theology of the Church	4 Foundations for Christian Mission
The Word That Creates The Word That Convicts The Word That Converts The Word That Calls	God's Reign Challenged God's Reign Inaugurated God's Reign Invading God's Reign Consummated	The Church Foreshadowed in God's Plan The Church at Worship The Church as Witness The Church at Work	The Vision and Biblical Foundation for Christian Mission I The Vision and Biblical Foundation for Christian Mission II Christian Mission and the City Christian Mission and the Poor
5 Bible Interpretation	6 God the Father	7 Foundations of Christian Leadership	8 Evangelism and Spiritual Warfare
Biblical Inspiration: The Origins and Authority of the Bible Biblical Hermeneutics: The Three-Step Model Biblical Literature: Interpreting the Genres of the Bible Biblical Studies: Using Study Tools in Bible Study	Prolegomena: The Doctrine of God and the Advance of the Kingdom God as Creator: The Providence of God The Triune God: The Greatness of God God as Father: The Goodness of God	The Christian Leader as Deacon The Christian Leader as Elder The Christian Leader as Pastor The Christian Leader as Bishop	Spiritual Warfare: Binding of the Strong Man Evangelism: The Content of the Good News of the Kingdom Evangelism: Methods to Reach the Urban Community Follow-up and Incorporation
9 The Old Testament Witness to Christ and His Kingdom	10 God the Son	11 Practicing Christian Leadership	12 Focus on Reproduction
The Promise Given The Promise Clarified The Promise Personalized The Promise Universalized	Jesus, Messiah and Lord of All: He Came Jesus, Messiah and Lord of All: He Lived Jesus, Messiah and Lord of All: He Died Jesus, Messiah and Lord of All: He Rose and Will Return	Effective Worship Leading: Worship, Word, and Sacrament Effective Christian Education: Incorporating, Parenting, and Discipling Effective Church Discipline: Exhorting, Rebuking, and Restoring Effective Counseling: Preparing, Caring, and Healing	Church Growth: Reproducing in Number and Quality Planting Urban Churches: Sowing Planting Urban Churches: Tending Planting Urban Churches: Reaping
13 The New Testament Witness to Christ and His Kingdom	14 God the Holy Spirit	15 The Equipping Ministry	16 Doing Justice and Loving Mercy: Compassion Ministries
The Messiah Announced The Messiah Opposed The Messiah Revealed The Messiah Vindicated	The Person of the Holy Spirit The Prophetic Work of the Holy Spirit The Powerful Presence of the Holy Spirit I The Powerful Presence of the Holy Spirit II	The Ministry of Proclamation: Kerygma I The Ministry of Proclamation: Kerygma II The Ministry of Teaching: Didache I The Ministry of Teaching: Didache II	Let Justice Roll Down: The Vision and Theology of the Kingdom Doing Justice and Loving Mercy I: The Urban Congregation Doing Justice and Loving Mercy II: Urban Community and Neighborhood Doing Justice and Loving Mercy III: Society and World

Source: *Planting Churches among the City's Poor, Volume 2,* pp. 119-125

Fit to Represent: Multiplying Disciples of the Kingdom of God

Rev. Dr. Don L. Davis

Luke 10.16 (ESV) - The one who hears you hears me, and the one who rejects you rejects me, and the one who rejects me rejects him who sent me.

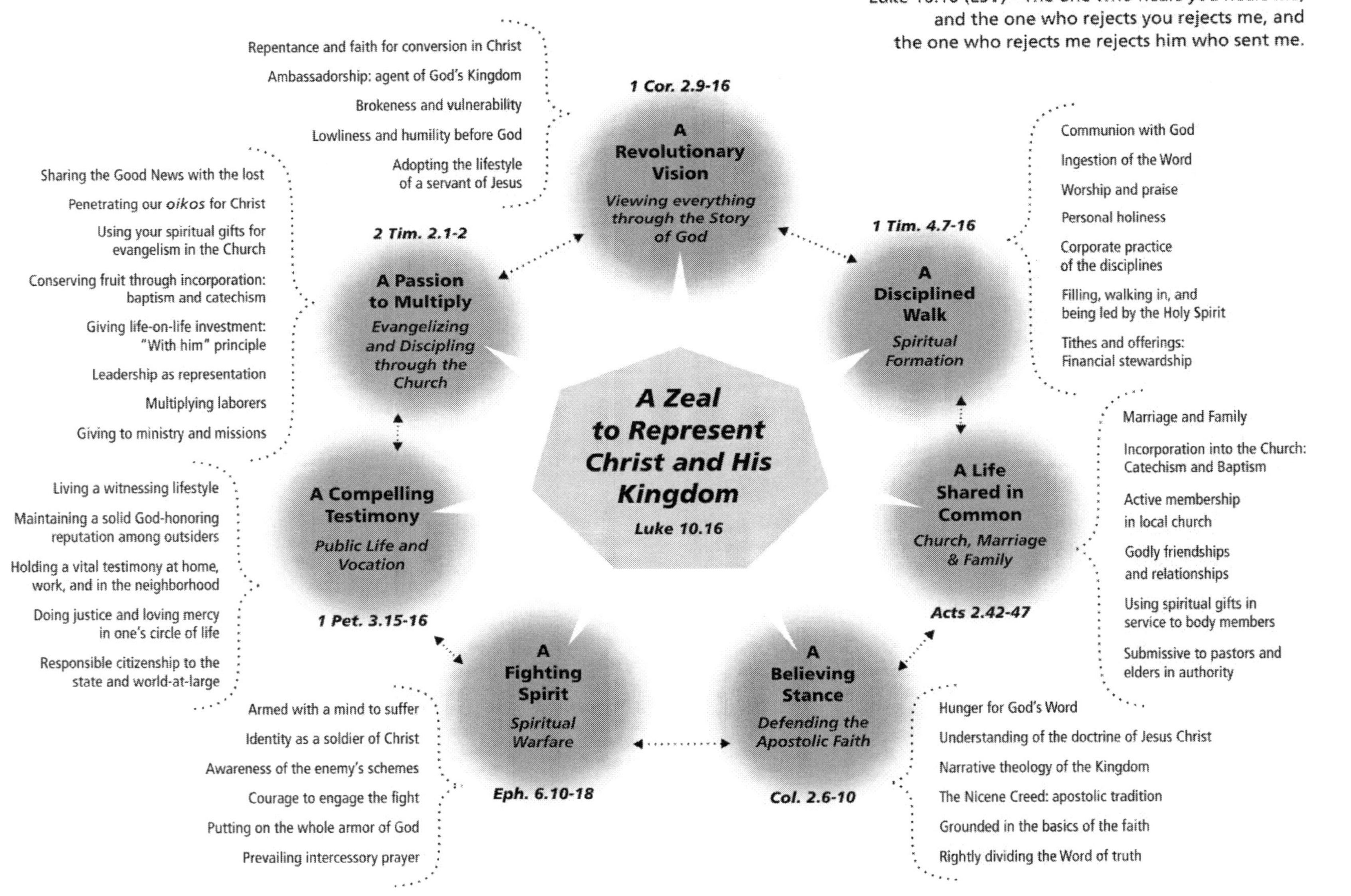

Source: *Planting Churches among the City's Poor, Volume 2*, p. 197

Discipling the Faithful

Establishing Leaders for the Urban Church

Rev. Dr. Don L. Davis

	Commission	Character	Competence	Community
Definition	Recognizes *the call of God* and replies with prompt obedience to his lordship and leading	Reflects *the character of Christ* in his/her personal convictions, conduct, and lifestyle	Responds in *the power of the Spirit* with excellence in carrying out their appointed tasks and ministry	Regards multiplying disciples in *the body of Christ* as the primary role of ministry
Key Scripture	2 Tim. 1.6-14; 1 Tim. 4.14; Acts 1.8; Matt. 28.18-20	John 15.4-5; 2 Tim. 2.2; 1 Cor. 4.2; Gal. 5.16-23	2 Tim. 2.15; 3.16-17; Rom. 15.14; 1 Cor. 12	Eph. 4.9-15; 1 Cor. 12.1-27
Critical Concept	The Authority of **God**: God's leader acts on God's recognized call and authority, acknowledged by the saints and God's leaders	The Humility of **Christ**: God's leader demonstrates the mind and lifestyle of Christ in his or her actions and relationships	The Power of the **Spirit**: God's leader operates in the gifting and anointing of the Holy Spirit	The Growth of the **Church**: God's leader uses all of his or her resources to equip and empower the body of Christ for his/her goal and task
Central Elements	A clear call from God Authentic testimony before God and others Deep sense of personal conviction based on Scripture Personal burden for a particular task or people Confirmation by leaders and the body	Passion for Christlikeness Radical lifestyle for the Kingdom Serious pursuit of holiness Discipline in the personal life Fulfills role-relationships and bond-slave of Jesus Christ Provides an attractive model for others in their conduct, speech, and lifestyle (the fruit of the Spirit)	Endowments and gifts from the Spirit Sound discipling from an able mentor Skill in the spiritual disciplines Ability in the Word Able to evangelize, follow up, and disciple new converts Strategic in the use of resources and people to accomplish God's task	Genuine love for and desire to serve God's people Disciples faithful individuals Facilitates growth in small groups Pastors and equips believers in the congregation Nurtures associations and networks among Christians and churches Advances new movements among God's people locally
Satanic Strategy to Abort	Operates on the basis of personality or position rather than on God's appointed call and ongoing authority	Substitutes ministry activity and/or hard work and industry for godliness and Christlikeness	Functions on natural gifting and personal ingenuity rather than on the Spirit's leading and gifting	Exalts tasks and activities above equipping the saints and developing Christian community
Key Steps	Identify God's call Discover your burden Be confirmed by leaders	Abide in Christ Discipline for godliness Pursue holiness in all	Discover the Spirit's gifts Receive excellent training Hone your performance	Embrace God's Church Learn leadership's contexts Equip concentrically
Results	Deep confidence in God arising from God's call	Powerful Christlike example provided for others to follow	Dynamic working of the Holy Spirit	Multiplying disciples in the Church

Source: *Planting Churches among the City's Poor, Volume 1*, p. 375

Understanding Leadership as Representation: The Six Stages of Formal Proxy

Rev. Dr. Don L. Davis

Luke 10.1 (ESV) – After this the Lord appointed seventy-two others and sent them on ahead of him, two by two, into every town and place where he himself was about to go . . .

Luke 10.16 (ESV) – "The one who hears you hears me, and the one who rejects you rejects me,and the one who rejects me rejects him who sent me."

John 20.21 (ESV) – Jesus said to them again, "Peace be with you. As the Father has sent me, even so I am sending you."

CONSCIENCE
CONVICTION
CHARACTER

The Revealed Will of God

Leadership As Representation

Consent of Your Leaders

The Fulfillment of the Task and Mission

Commissioning (1)

Formal Selection and Call to Represent

- Chosen to be an emissary, envoy, or proxy
- Confirmed by appropriate other who recognize the call
- Is recognized to be a member of a faithful community
- Calling out of a group to a particular role of representation
- Calling to a particular task or mission
- Delegation of position or responsibility

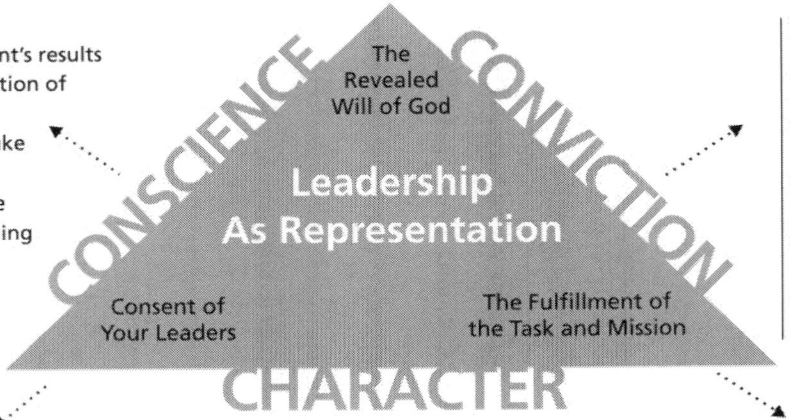

Equipping (2)

Appropriate Resourcing and Training to Fulfill the Call

- Assignment to a supervisor, superior, mentor, or instructor
- Disciplined instruction of principles underlying the call
- Constant drill, practice, and exposure to appropriate skills
- Recognition of gifts and strengths
- Expert coaching and ongoing feedback

Entrustment (3)

Corresponding Authorization and Empowerment to Act

- Delegation of authority to act and speak on commissioner's behalf
- Scope and limits of representative power provided
- Formal deputization (right to enforce and represent)
- Permission given to be an emissary (to stand in stead of)
- Release to fulfill the commission and task received

Mission (4)

Faithful and Disciplined Engagement of the Task

- Subordination of one's will to accomplish the assignment
- Obedience: carrying out the orders of those who sent you
- Fulfilling the task that was given to you
- Freely acting within one's delegated authority to fulfill the task
- Maintaining loyalty to those who sent you
- Using all means available to do one's duty, whatever the cost
- Full recognition of one's answerability to the one(s) who commissioned

Reckoning (5)

Official Evaluation and Review of One's Execution

- Reporting back to sending authority for critical review
- Formal comprehensive assessment of one's execution and results
- Judgment of one's loyalties and faithfulness
- Sensitive analysis of what we accomplished
- Readiness to ensure that our activities and efforts produce results

Reward (6)

Public Recognition and Continuing Response

- Formal publishing of assessment's results
- Acknowledgment and recognition of behavior and conduct
- Corresponding reward or rebuke for execution
- Review made basis for possible reassignment or recommissioning
- Assigning new projects with greater authority

Source: *Planting Churches among the City's Poor, Volume 2*, p. 66

Source: *The Evangel Dean Handbook,* pp. 201-208

Overview of TUMI's Resources on the Urban Poor

The Urban Ministry Institute (TUMI) has developed more than seven hundred resources for equipping church leaders to engage in urban ministry and mission. Currently these resources are being used in hundreds of churches and urban ministries around the globe. The resources fall into three categories: Church Planting, Spiritual Formation and Discipleship, and Leadership Development.

I. Church Planting

A. What resource is the single most important practical tool for World Impact Church Plant Coaches and Team Leaders?

1. Don Allsman, Don L. Davis, and Hank Voss, eds., *Ripe for Harvest: A Guidebook for Planting Healthy Churches in the City.* Wichita, KS: TUMI Press, 2015.

2. Our Evangel School of Urban Church Planting trains church planters to plant healthy churches among the city's poor, applying biblical wisdom in order to effectively evangelize, equip, and empower unreached city folk to respond to the love of Christ, and take their place in representing Christ's Kingdom where they live and work. This guidebook, the official text of the Evangel School, outlines a process of church planting that respects the unique cultures, environments, communities, and situations reflected in urban America. The PLANT approach outlined here provides practically wise and spiritually vital instruction for urban church planting teams. Filled with devotionals, seminars, exercises, and worksheets, with dozens of graphics, diagrams, and articles, this rich resource will empower church planting teams to design a strategy consistent with the vision God has given them – the kind of strategy that results in the creation of healthy, Kingdom-declaring churches, and the launch of reproducing church planting movements.

Source: *The Evangel Dean Handbook,* pp. 201-208

B. What are the two most important theological books for WI Church Planters?

1. Davis, Don. *Sacred Roots: A Primer on Retrieving the Great Tradition*. Wichita, KS: The Urban Ministry Institute, 2010.

2. Smith, Efrem. *The Post-Black and Post-White Church: Becoming the Beloved Community in a Multi-Ethnic World.* Vol. 59. San Francisco: Jossey-Bass, 2012.

C. What is the most important supplementary resource produced by TUMI for urban church planters and coaches?

1. Don L. Davis, ed., *Planting Churches among the City's Poor: An Anthology of Urban Church Planting Resources, Volume 1: Theological and Missiological Perspectives for Church Planters*. Wichita, KS: TUMI Press, 2015.

2. Don L. Davis, ed., *Planting Churches among the City's Poor: An Anthology of Urban Church Planting Resources, Volume 2: Resources and Tools for Coaches and Teams*. Wichita, KS: TUMI Press, 2015.

3. This two-volume set (with nearly 1,000 pages of resources) is an anthology of much of our research, dialogue, and insight gleaned over the past two decades of church planting among the poor. It is a comprehensive collection of diverse materials, covering numerous topics and issues, all designed to help you better understand the theological, missiological, cultural, and anthropological roots of valid church planting work in the city. For those interested in church planting among the city's neediest population, this set is an absolute must.

D. How many courses are available from TUMI on Church Planting?

1. *Focus on Reproduction*

   a. One of four Capstone Curriculum Urban Missions Courses, this eight segment course covers the foundational principles of church planting.

   b. This is the most important course available for WI Church Planters.

Source:
The Evangel Dean Handbook, pp. 201-208

2. *Winning the World*

    a. The focus of the course is on Church Plant Movements.

    b. This course can be downloaded and taken for free at *www.biblicaltraining.org*.

3. *Vision for Mission: Nurturing an Apostolic Heart*

    a. A TUMI Foundations Class.

    b. Significantly impacted numerous World Impact missionaries to pursue church planting. *http://www.tumistore.org/foundations-nurturing-an-apostolic-heart-course/*

E. What is Evangel Church Plant School?

1. World Impact's church plant schools have chartered more than eighty church plant teams. The next one is tentatively planned for November, 2015. Watch for more information on the Evangel Church Plant School.

2. Look for *Evangel Church Plant School* at a location near you. Contact Hank Voss if you or a church plant team leader you know is interested in a school in your region (*hvoss@worldimpact.org*).

F. What system was used to train World Impact missionaries, church planters, team leaders and church plant team coaches from 2000 through 2007?

1. The *John Mark Curriculum*. This five hundred page resource provided thirty three training modules on discreet topics related to urban mission including modules on Culture, Counseling, Evangelism, Team Leadership, Coaching a Church Plant Team, etc.

2. This resource is now out of print although hard copies are available in all WI cities.

Source: *The Evangel Dean Handbook,* pp. 201-208

G. What is a sample resource developed by a World Impact Church Plant?

1. Christ the Victor is a church in the Midwest region that has started reproducing church plants. Its Church Resource Guidebook is available from Amazon.

2. Contact Ryan Carter (*rcarter@worldimpact.org*) for more on Christ the Victor resources, church planting conferences, etc.

H. In 2015 look for two new manuals on church planting to be released by The Urban Ministry Institute.

II. Spiritual Formation and Discipleship

A. Sermons and preaching resources

1. More than 500 sermons, lectures, and conference presentations are available for free download at two TUMI websites:

a. As of October 10, 2014 there are 72 sermons available for download at *https://soundcloud.com/tumimedia/sets*

b. At *http://www.tumimedia.org*

(1) More than 450 sermons, lectures and conference presentations

(2) More than 90 topics are addressed and can be searched easily using topical search tool

2. What kind of series are available for free download?

a. Revised Common Lectionary Year A (more than fifty sermons)

b. Revised Common Lectionary Year B (more than fifty sermons)

c. Revised Common Lectionary Year C (more than fifty sermons)

Source:
The Evangel Dean Handbook,
pp. 201-208

d. Effective Worship Leading (12 audio messages) found at *www.tumimedia.org*.

e. Revelation (22 Sermons), and many more.

B. Songs and Worship Resources

1. Dr. Davis has written more than 1,500 songs, many of which are available for free. (As of October 10, 2014 there are 44 songs and soundtracks available for free download at *https://soundcloud.com/tumimedia/sets.)*

2. Listen to the twelve-session course on *Effective Worship Leading* at *www.tumimedia.org*. See also the TUMI's technical resource for learning the guitar entitled *Making Joyful Noises*.

C. Spiritual discipline resources

1. TUMI Annual (*http://www.tumistore.org/church-resources/*)

   a. A devotional guide to prayer and reading Scripture, published every year by TUMI

   b. Each year focuses on a different theme.

2. TUMI Calendar (*http://www.tumistore.org/church-resources/*)

   a. TUMI's Scripture texts for the preaching, reading, and prayer taken from the RCL each year

   b. Each year redesigned with new artwork

3. Master the Bible (*http://www.tumistore.org/master-the-bible/*)

   a. Four-year plan to memorize more than 800 scripture passages. See a review at *http://www.tumi.org/forum/showthread.php?t=80*

   b. Resource for churches to plan how to help their people memorize Scripture. Includes, book, dvds, bookmarks, posters

Source: *The Evangel Dean Handbook,* pp. 201-208

4. Prayer Resources

   a. Prayer Mountain! Free Retreat Center at World Impact's Oaks Conference Center for all church planters taking a personal spiritual retreat

   b. Let God Arise Prayer Network Resources

      (1) Don Davis, *Let God Arise* (TUMI, 2000)

      (2) *www.letgodarise.com*

D. Discipleship Resources

1. *Fight the Good Fight: Playing Your Part in God's Unfolding Drama* is now available (Jan 1, 2015). It is a new believers follow-up curriculum based on the book of Ephesians and can be purchased at *http://www.tumistore.org/fight-the-good-fight/*.

2. *Fit to Represent: Vision for Discipleship Seminar* is available now at *http://www.tumistore.org/fit-to-represent-vision-for-discipleship-seminar/*.

E. What are the best Men's and Women's Discipleship tools developed by TUMI and World Impact to date? (*http://www.tumi.org/siafu*)

1. Don Davis. *The SIAFU Network Guidebook: Standing Together for Christ in the City.* TUMI, 2013.

2. Don Davis. *The SIAFU Chapter Meeting Guide*. TUMI, 2013.

F. More than 700 resources developed for urban churches and leaders engaged in urban ministry available at *www.tumistore.org* and at *http://www.cafepress.com/tumi*.

1. Resources include artwork, videos, clothing, books, etc.

2. More than 30 resources available in Spanish

Source: *The Evangel Dean Handbook,* pp. 201-208

III. Leadership Development

A. Books

1. Don Davis. *Sacred Roots: A Primer on Retrieving the Great Tradition*. Wichita, KS: The Urban Ministry Institute, 2010.

2. Don Allsman. *Jesus Cropped from the Picture: Why Christians Get Bored and How to Restore Them to Vibrant Faith*. Wichita, KS: The Urban Ministry Institute, 2010.

3. Efrem Smith. *The Post-Black and Post-White Church: Becoming the Beloved Community in a Multi-Ethnic World*. Vol. 59, Jossey-Bass Leadership Network Series. San Francisco: Jossey-Bass, 2012.

B. Leadership Development Classes

1. The Urban Ministry Institute Satellite (TUMI) Network

   a. Currently more than 180 urban ministries, churches, and denominations have launched TUMI leadership training institutes for training leaders in their ministry context.

   b. Learn how to start a satellite at your ministry by visiting *www.tumi.org/satellite*.

2. The Capstone Curriculum

   a. TUMI's premier leadership training program. Sixteen classes usually taken over a four year period with courses in four subject areas: Biblical Studies; Christian Ministry; Urban Mission; and Christian Theology.

   b. The Capstone Courses can be transferred to several accredited colleges and universities for those interested in continuing their education. For more information on Capstone, visit *www.tumi.org/capstone*.

3. Foundations courses (13 currently available)

   a. Sample courses include *Church Matters*. A course that covers the major periods of the church and emphasizes how evangelical churches can be renewed by a retrieval of the Great Tradition and the pursuit of a shared

Source:
The Evangel Dean Handbook,
pp. 201-208

spirituality. *http://www.tumistore.org/foundations-church-matters-course/*

b. Sample Courses include *Marking Time: Forming Spirituality through the Christian Year*. This course introduces evangelicals to a theology of time rooted in the practice of the Christian Year. The course looks at the way a shared spirituality can equip churches working among the poor with vital resources for discipleship, preaching, and worship. *http://www.tumistore.org/foundations-marking-time-course/*

C. Conferences

1. Annual TUMI Summit. More than two hundred leaders from around the globe who are involved with urban leadership development through the TUMI satellite network. Find more information at *www.tumi.org/satellite*.

2. Men's and Women's SIAFU Conferences. Regional men's and women's conferences to encourage missional outreach in the cities. See *http://www.tumi.org/siafu* for more information.

An Abridged Church Planting Bibliography

Source: *Planting Churches among the City's Poor, Volume 1,* pp. 513-518

An Abridged Church Planting Bibliography

The Urban Ministry Institute

Allen, Roland. *Missionary Methods: St. Paul's or Ours?* Grand Rapids: Wm. B. Eerdmans Publishing Company, 2001.

Arn, Win, and Charles Arn. *The Master's Plan for Making Disciples*, 2nd ed. Grand Rapids: Baker Books, 1998.

Banks, Robert. *Paul's Idea of Community*, rev. ed. Peabody, MA: Hendrickson Publishers, 1994.

Becker, Paul. *Dynamic Church Planting: A Complete Handbook*. Vista, Calif.: Multiplication Ministries, 1992.

Bessenecker, Scott A. *Overturning Tables: Freeing Missions from the Christian-Industrial Complex*. Downers Grover, IL: InterVarsity Press, 2014.

Black, Vicki K. *Welcome to the Church Year: An Introduction to the Seasons of the Episcopal Church*. Harrisburg, PA: Morehouse Publishing, 2004.

Carter, Ryan, ed. *Christ the Victor Church: The Guidebook: Ancient Faith for an Urban Movement*. N.P.: CreateSpace, 2014.

Chaney, Charles L. *Church Planting at the End of the Twentieth Century*. Revised and expanded. Wheaton: Tyndale House Publishers, 1991.

Conn, Harvie M. *Planting and Growing Urban Churches: From Dream to Reality*. Grand Rapids, MI: Baker Books, 1997.

Davis, Don L. *Vision for Mission: Nurturing an Apostolic Heart*. Wichita, KS: The Urban Ministry Institute (World Impact, Inc.), 1999.

———. *Focus on Reproduction*. Vol. 12, 16 vols. *The Capstone Curriculum*. Wichita, KS: The Urban Ministry Institute (World Impact, Inc.), 2005.

———. *Marking Time. Forming Spirituality through the Christian Year*. Wichita, KS: The Urban Ministry Institute (World Impact, Inc.), 2007.

———. *Ministry in a Multi-Cultural and Unchurched Society*. Wichita, KS: The Urban Ministry Institute (World Impact, Inc.), 2007.

Source: *Planting Churches among the City's Poor, Volume 1,* pp. 513-518

———. *Winning the World: Facilitating Urban Church Planting Movements*. Wichita, KS: The Urban Ministry Institute (World Impact, Inc.), 2007.

———. *Master the Bible Guidebook: Charting Your Course through Scripture Memorization*. Wichita, KS: The Urban Ministry Institute (World Impact, Inc.), 2008.

———. *Church Matters: Retrieving the Great Tradition*. Wichita, KS: The Urban Ministry Institute (World Impact, Inc.), 2010.

———. *Sacred Roots: A Primer on Retrieving the Great Tradition*. Wichita, KS: The Urban Ministry Institute (World Impact, Inc.), 2010.

———. *The Most Amazing Story Ever Told*. Wichita, KS: The Urban Ministry Institute (World Impact, Inc.), 2011.

Davis, Don L. and Terry Cornett. *The Capstone Curriculum*. 16 vols. Wichita, KS: The Urban Ministry Institute (World Impact, Inc.) 2005.

ETA (Evangelical Training Association). *Perspectives from Church History*. Wheaton, IL: Evangelical Training Association, 1996.

Fairchild, Samuel D. *Church Planting for Reproduction*. Grand Rapids: Baker Book House, 1991.

Francis, Hozell C. *Church Planting in the African-American Context*. Grand Rapids, MI: Zondervan Publishing House, 1999.

Garrison, David. *Church Planting Movements*. Midlothian, VA: WIGTake Resources, 2004.

Gonzales, Justo L. *Church History: An Essential Guide*. Nashville: Abingdon Press, 1996.

Greenway, Roger S., and Timothy M. Monsma. *Cities: Missions' New Frontier*, 2nd Ed. Grand Rapids, MI: Baker Books, 2000.

Hauerwas, Stanley and Willian H. Willimon. *Resident Aliens: Life in the Christian Colony*. Nashville, TN: Abingdon Press, 1989.

Source: *Planting Churches among the City's Poor, Volume 1*, pp. 513-518

Hesselgrave, David J. *Planting Churches Cross-Culturally*, 2nd Ed. Grand Rapids, MI: Baker Books, 2000.

Hickman, Hoyt L, Don E. Saliers, Laurence Hull Stookey, James F. White. *The New Handbook of the Christian Year*. Nashville, TN: Abingdon Press, 1992.

Hiebert, Paul G. *Anthropological Insights for Missionaries*. Grand Rapids, MI: Baker Books, 1985.

Hiebert, Paul G. and Eloise Hiebert Meneses. *Incarnational Ministry: Planting Churches in Band, Tribal, Peasant, and Urban Societies*. Grand Rapids, MI: Baker Books, 1995.

Jennings, Willie James. *The Christian Imagination: Theology and the Origins of Race*. New Haven: Yale University Press, 2010.

Kreider, Larry. *House Church Networks*. Ephrata, PA: House to House Publications, 2001.

Kyle, John E. ed. *Urban Mission: God's Concern for the City*. Downers Grove, IL: InterVarsity Press, 1988.

Ladd, G. E. *Gospel of the Kingdom*. Grand Rapids, MI: Eerdmans, 1959.

Liele, George. "An Account of Several Baptist Churches, Consisting Chiefly of Negro Slaves: Particularly of One at Kingston, in Jamaica; and Another at Savannah in Georgia (1793)." In *Unchained Voices: An Anthology of Black Authors in the English-speaking World of the Eighteenth Century*. Edited by Vincent Carretta. Lexington: University Press of Kentucky, 2004.

———. "The Covenant of the Anabaptist Church: Began in America 1777, in Jamaica, Dec. 1783." 1796. British Baptist material, Angus Library of Regents Park College, Oxford, England, reel 1, no. 14.; Publication (Historical Commission, Southern Baptist Convention), MF # 4265.

Liele, George and Andrew Bryan. "Letters from Pioneer Black Baptists." In *Afro-American Religious History: A Documentary Witness*. Edited by Milton C. Sernett. Durham, NC: Duke University Press, 1985.

Source:
Planting Churches among the City's Poor, Volume 1, pp. 513-518

———. "Letters Showing the Rise and Progress of the Early Negro Churches of Georgia and the West Indies." Comprised of "An Account of Several Baptist Churches, Consisting Chiefly of Negro Slaves: Particularly of One at Kingston, in Jamaica; and Another at Savannah in Georgia," and "Sketches of the Black Baptist Church at Savannah, in Georgia: And of Their Minister Andrew Bryan, Extracted from Several Letters." *Journal of Negro History* 1 no. 1 (Jan. 1916): 69-92.

Logan, Robert E., and Steven L. Ogne. *Church Planter's Toolkit.* Pasadena: Charles E. Fuller Institute of Evangelism & Church Growth, 1991.

Logan, Robert E., and Neil Cole. *Beyond Church Planting: Pathways for Emerging Churches.* St. Charles, IL: ChurchSmart Resources, 2005.

Malphurs, Aubrey. *Planting Growing Churches for the 21st Century: A Comprehensive Guide for New Churches and Those Desiring Renewal.* 2nd ed. Grand Rapids: Baker Books, 1998.

Mannoia, Kevin. *Church Planting the Next Generation: Introducing the Century 21 Church Planting System.* Indianapolis: Light and Life Press, 1994.

Miley, George. *Loving the Church, Blessing the Nations: Pursuing the Role of Local Churches in Global Mission.* Waynesboro, GA: Authentic Media, 2003.

Montgomery, Jim. *DAWN 2000: 7 Million Churches to Go.* Pasadena: William Carey Library, 1989.

Mull, Marlin. *A Biblical Church Planting Manual from the Book of Acts.* Eugene, OR: Wipf and Stock Publishers, 2003.

Nebel, Tom, and Gary Rohrmayer. *Church Planting Landmines: Mistakes to Avoid in Years 2 through 10.* St. Charles, IL: ChurchSmart Resources.

Niebuhr, H. Richard. *Christ and Culture.* New York, NY: HarperSanFrancisco, 1951.

Noll, Mark A. *Turning Points: Decisive Moments in the History of Christianity.* Grand Rapids, MI: Baker Academic (Baker Book House), 1997, 2000.

Source: *Planting Churches among the City's Poor, Volume 1,* pp. 513-518

Overstreet, Don. *Sent Out: The Calling, the Character, and the Challenge of the Apostle/Missionary*. Bloomington, IN: Crossbooks, 2009.

Overstreet, Don, and Mark Hammond. *God's Call to the City*. Bloomington, IN: Crossbooks, 2011.

Phillips, Keith. *Out of Ashes*. Los Angeles, CA: World Impact Press, 1996.

Ratliff, Joe S., and Michael J. Cox. *Church Planting in the African-American Community*. Nashville: Broadman Press, 1993.

Romo, Oscar I. American Mosaic: *Church Planting in Ethnic America.* Nashville: Broadman Press, 1993.

Schaller, Lyle. *44 Questions for Church Planters*. Nashville: Abingdon Press, 1991.

Schwarz, Christian A. *Natural Church Development*. St. Charles, IL: ChurchSmart Resources, 2000.

Searcy, Nelson, and Kerrick Thomas. *Launch: Starting a New Church from Scratch*. Ventura, Calif.: Regal Books, 2007.

Shenk, David W., and Ervin R. Stutzman. *Creating Communities of the Kingdom: New Testament Models of Church Planting*. Scottdale: Herald Press, 1988.

Smith, Efrem. *Raising Up Young Heroes: Developing a Revolutionary Youth Ministry*. Downers Grove: InterVarsity Press, 2004.

———. *Jump into a Life of Further and Higher*. Colorado Springs: David C. Cook, 2010.

———. *The Post-Black and Post-White Church: Becoming the Beloved Community in a Multi-Ethnic World*. San Francisco: Jossey-Bass Publishers, 2012.

Smith, Efrem and Phil Jackson. *The Hip-Hop Church: Connecting with the Movement Shaping our Culture*. Downers Grove: InterVarsity Press, 2005.

Snyder, Howard A. *Kingdom, Church, and World*. Eugene, OR: Wipf and Stock, 1997.

Source: *Planting Churches among the City's Poor, Volume 1,* pp. 513-518

———. *The Community of the King*, Rev. ed. Downers Grove, IL: InterVarsity Press, 2004.

Stetzer, Ed. *Planting New Churches in a Postmodern Age*. Nashville: Broadman & Holman Publishers, 2003.

———. *Planting Missional Chruches*. Nashville: B & H Publishing Group, 2006.

———. "Books/Resources on Ethnic Groups in the U.S. and Canada." *The Exchange*. April 15, 2008. *http://www.christianitytoday.com/edstetzer*.

———. "Church Planting Bibliography." *The Exchange*. April 20, 2009. *http://www.christianitytoday.com/edstetzer*.

Surratt, Geoff, Greg Ligon, and Warren Bird. *The Multi-Site Church Revolution: Being One Church in Many Locations*. Grand Rapids: Zondervan, 2006.

Teja, Gary, and John Wagenveld, eds. *Planting Healthy Churches*. Sauk Village, IL: Multiplication Network Ministries, 2015.

Wagner, C. Peter. *Church Planting for a Greater Harvest: A Comprehensive Guide*. Ventura: Regal Books, 1990.

Webber, Robert E. *Ancient-Future Time: Forming Spirituality through the Christian Year*. Grand Rapids, MI: Baker Books, 2004.

Woodson, Carter Godwin. *The History of the Negro Church*. Washington, D.C.: Associated Publishers, 1921.

Appendix: World Impact's Church Planting Resources at a Glance

The following pages list the actual *Table of Contents* contained in each of the four volumes whose materials are represented in this sampler. These documents allow you to see the full scope and breadth of the materials included in the four works which contain World Impact's resources on church planting, church planting movements, and church development.

- **Table of Contents:** *Ripe for Harvest*
- **Table of Contents:** *Planting Churches among the City's Poor, Volume 1*
- **Table of Contents:** *Planting Churches among the City's Poor, Volume 2*
- **Prologue:** *Planting Churches among the City's Poor, Volumes 1 and 2*
- **Table of Contents:** *The Evangel Dean Handbook*

Table of Contents:
Ripe for Harvest

Preface: How to Use This Guidebook 11

Introduction:
Sacred Roots, Church Planting, and the Great Tradition . . 23

Session 1: Seeing the Big Picture 29

Worship and Devotional

The Power of Praise 33

Session Themes and Objectives 43

Seminar Teaching

Seminar 1:
What Is a Church? 47

Seminar 2:
Church Planting Overview 51

Seminar 3:
Using Wisdom in Ministry: The PWR Process 62

Team Exercises:
Establishing Context

Exercise Guidelines 77

Exercise Instructions 79

Exercise Readings

A Call to an Ancient Evangelical Future 81

Church Planting Models 85

Team Exercises:
Defining Values/Vision

Exercise Guidelines 91

Exercise Instructions 93

Team Exercises 94

Charting Your Own Course 103

Resources for Further Study 107

Appendix Listing 111

Table of Contents:
Ripe for Harvest

Session 2: Prepare: "P" 113

Worship and Devotional

Freedom in Christ 117

Session Themes and Objectives 131

Seminar Teaching

Seminar 1:
The Difference That Difference Makes:
Culture, Religion, and Diversity in Post-Modern Society . . . 135

Seminar 2:
The Theology of the Poor for Church Planters 155

Seminar 3:
Building the Team for Success:
Principles of Effective Team Play 169

Team Exercises
Prepare: Be the Church

Overview of Exercise Phases for
World Impact's Evangel School of Urban Church Planting . . 186

Exercise Guidelines 188

Exercise Instructions 190

Exercise Questions 191

Exercise Readings

On World Impact's "Empowering the Urban Poor" . . . 195

Responding to God's Call to the Poor 201

As You Form Your Plan, Keep Your Overall Purpose in Mind: To Cross-Culturally Plant an Indigenously Led Reproducing Church among Residents of a Low-Income Community . . 203

Key Roles of a Church Planting Team 205

Charting Your Own Course 209

Resources for Further Study 213

Appendix Listing 217

Table of Contents:
Ripe for Harvest

Session 3: Launch and Assemble: "L" and "A" . . 219

Worship and Devotional

Prayer Is the Walkie-Talkie of Faith 223

Session Themes and Objectives 233

Seminar Teaching

Seminar 1:
Evangelism and Follow-up as Mission:
Incorporation into the Body of Christ 237

Seminar 2:
Christus Victor: An Ancient Biblical Motif for Connecting the Dots in Urban Spiritual Formation and Cross-Cultural Missions . 249

Seminar 3:
Conducting Events and Projects 275

Team Exercises
Launch: Expand the Church

Overview of Exercise Phases for
World Impact's Evangel School of Urban Church Planting . . 286

Exercise Guidelines 288

Exercise Instructions 289

Exercise Questions 290

Team Exercises
Assemble: Establish the Church

Overview of Exercise Phases for
World Impact's Evangel School of Urban Church Planting . . 294

Exercise Guidelines 296

Exercise Instructions 297

Exercise Questions 298

Exercise Readings

Welcome to the Family:
Membership Responsibilities and Leadership 301

Charting Your Own Course 325

Resources for Further Study 329

Appendix Listing 333

Table of Contents:
Ripe for Harvest

Session 4: Nurture and Transition: "N" and "T" . 337

Worship and Devotional

God Is a Warrior 341

Session Themes and Objectives 355

Seminar Teaching

Seminar 1:
Effective Discipling in the Church 359

Seminar 2:
Discipling Urban Christian Leaders 377

Seminar 3:
Preaching and Teaching: The Fine Art of Communicating the Truth . 383

Seminar 4:
Selecting a Credible Criteria for Independence:
Navigating Toward a Healthy Transition 394

Team Exercises
Nurture: Mature the Church

Overview of Exercise Phases for
World Impact's Evangel School of Urban Church Planting . . 400

Exercise Guidelines 402

Exercise Instructions 403

Exercise Questions 404

Exercise Readings

The Dynamic Dozen:
Foundational Principles of the Nurture Phase 406

Drafting a Constitution (Bylaws):
Key Tool for Nurturing Community 410

Nurture and Transition Dimensions 411

Team Exercises
Transition: Release the Church

Overview of Exercise Phases for
World Impact's Evangel School of Urban Church Planting . . 414

Exercise Guidelines 416

Exercise Instructions 417

Exercise Questions 419

Exercise Readings

The Self-Governing Seven:
Central Principles for the Transition Phase 421

Transition 424

Table of Contents:
Ripe for Harvest

Charting Your Own Course 429

Resources for Further Study 433

Appendix Listing 437

Session 5: Bringing It All Together ***439***

Worship and Devotional

Adapt to Win 443

Session Themes and Objectives 453

Seminar Teaching

Seminar 1:
Selecting a Credible Criteria for Independence:
Navigating Toward a Healthy Transition 457

Team Exercises
Bringing It All Together

Overview of Exercise Phases for
World Impact's Evangel School of Urban Church Planting . . 462

Exercise Guidelines 464

Charting Your Own Course 471

Resources for Further Study 475

Appendix Listing 479

The Urban Ministry Institute:
Polishing the Stones That the Builders Reject –
How You Can Equip Leaders for
Your Church and Ministry ***483***

Table of Contents:

Planting Churches among the City's Poor, Volume 1

Prologue 11

Part I
Developing Urban Congregations:
A Framework for World Impact Church Planters . 19

Introduction. 21
World Impact and Church Planting 23
Theology of the Church 24
Modern Missions' History 28
Indigenous Churches 30
Multicultural Congregations 38
A Strategy for Planting Churches 43
Commission the Church-Planting Team 44
Cultivate the Community 50
Establish Discipling Fellowships 58
Form a Celebration Group 65
Plan the Finances 69
Provide Facilities 73
Constitute the Church 77
Church/Mission Relations 82
Conclusion 86
Bibliography 87

Table of Contents: *Planting Churches among the City's Poor, Volume 1*

Part II
Theological and Missiological Principles and Insights: Toward a Theology of Church Planting 93

Christus Victor: A Theology of the City and the Poor . . 95

The Theology of the Poor for Team Leaders 97

Ethics of the New Testament:
Living in the Upside-Down Kingdom of God 109

Christus Victor:
An Integrated Vision for the Christian Life and Witness . . . 110

The Kingdom of God: Church Planting in a Universe at War. . 111

Christus Victor: Toward a Biblical Theology for the Urban Church 120

Once upon a Time:
Understanding Our Church's Place in the Story of God . . . 150

The Black Church and Church Planting:
World Impact Blog, February 2015 163

A Theology of the Kingdom and the Church 167

Living in the Already and the Not Yet Kingdom 169

Jesus of Nazareth: The Presence of the Future 170

A Theology of the Church in Kingdom Perspective 171

A Schematic for a Theology of the Kingdom and the Church . 172

Thy Kingdom Come! Readings on the Kingdom of God . . . 173

There Is a River: Identifying the Streams of a
Revitalized Authentic Christian Community in the City . . . 182

The Role of Sound Ecclesiology in Urban Mission. 183

The Story of God: Our Sacred Roots 195

Substitute Centers to a Christ-Centered Vision: Goods and Effects
Which Our Culture Substitutes as the Ultimate Concern . . . 196

The Picture and the Drama:
Image and Story in the Recovery of Biblical Myth 197

Old Testament Witness to Christ and His Kingdom 198

The Theology of Christus Victor: A Christ-Centered Biblical
Motif for Integrating and Renewing the Urban Church . . . 199

The Theology of the Church for Team Leaders 200

Models of the Kingdom 209

Table of Contents:
Planting Churches among the City's Poor, Volume 1

A Theology of Christ and Culture 211

The Difference That Difference Makes:
Culture, Religion, and Diversity in Post-Modern Society . . . 213

Five Views of the Relationship between Christ and Culture . . 231

Interaction of Class, Culture, and Race 232

The Complexity of Difference: Race, Culture, Class 233

Cycle of Freedom 234

Authentic Freedom in Jesus Christ. 235

Too Legit to Quit: A Continuum of Cultural Practice 236

Apostolicity:
The Unique Place of the Apostles in Christian Faith and Practice 237

Theological Diversity 238

Creedal Theology as a Blueprint for Discipleship and Leadership:
A Time-Tested Criterion for Equipping New Believers
and Developing Indigenous Leaders 241

Translating the Story of God 253

Cross-Cultural Church Planting Principles 254

The Missionary Vocation: Assessing Cross-Cultural Adaptability. 255

Targeting Unreached Groups in Churched Neighborhoods . . 256

Different Traditions of African-American Response:
Interpreting a Legacy, Shaping an Identity, and
Pursuing a Destiny as a Minority Culture Person 257

Paul's Team Members:
Companions, Laborers, and Fellow Workers 260

Jesus' Practice of Silence and Solitude. 263

Seven Essential Practices for the Priesthood of All Believers . . 264

On World Impact's "Empowering the Urban Poor" 265

Responding to God's Call to the Poor 271

The Bible in Chronological Order: A Narrative
Literary Telling of the Story of God in Both Testaments . . . 273

From Before to Beyond Time:
The Plan of God and Human History 274

Table of Contents: *Planting Churches among the City's Poor, Volume 1*

Part III
Planting Urban Churches: Resources for Church Planters 277

Church Planting Movements Overview 279

Church Planting Overview 281
World Impact's Strategy for Church Planting 288
Mobilizing American Cities for Church Planting Movements . 292
Church Planting Movements, C1 Neighborhoods, and 80% Windows: The Importance of Vision 320
Discerning Valid Urban Church Planting Movements: Elements of Authentic Urban Christian Community 326

The Church Planter and the Church Plant Team 327

How to PLANT a Church 329
Responsibilities of a Church Plant Team Leader 336
The Heartbeat of a Church Planter: Discerning an Apostolic/Pastoral Identity 337
Practical Steps in Church Planting: Knowing Your Call and Your Community 349
Traditions (*Paradosis*) 356
What Shall I Preach, How Shall We Grow: The Urban Pastor's Dilemma 367
Forming the Church Plant Team and Understanding the Roles . 371
Discipling the Faithful: Establishing Leaders for the Urban Church 375
Spiritual Service Checklist 376

Models of Church Planting. 377

Overview PLANT to Birth Models 379
Three Levels of Ministry Investment 380
Six Types of Neighborhoods 381
Advancing the Kingdom in the City: Multiplying Congregations with a Common Identity. 382
Church Planting Models 385

Table of Contents: *Planting Churches among the City's Poor, Volume 1*

Overview of Church Plant Planning Phases 388
The Role of Women in Ministry 389
Ordination of Women Q and A 393
Defining the Leaders and Members of a Church Plant Team. . 396

Engaging the Community 397

Selecting a Target Area. 399
Researching Your Community 405
The *Oikos* Factor: Spheres of Relationship and Influence . . 418
Receptivity Scale 419
Living as an *Oikos* Ambassador 420
Apostolic Band: Cultivating Outreach for Dynamic Harvest . . 421
Resources for Studying Your Community 422
Ideas about Neighborhood Evangelism 423
Canvassing Dos and Don'ts. 424
Door-to-Door: Starting the Conversation 426

Body Life and Spiritual Formation. 427

Using Wisdom in Ministry: The PWR Process 429
Getting a Good Team Rhythm:
Time Management and Ministry Stewardship 439
Commissioning of Our Elders 442
Order of Service: Sample 1 444
Order of Service: Sample 2 445
Small Groups: Ten Principles and Their Implications
for Open Christian Gatherings. 455
The Service of Believer's Baptism 457
Sample Follow-up Card. 464
Church Plant Team Responsive Reading 465
Key Roles of a Church Planting Team 467
The Power of Multiplication: The 2 Timothy 2.2 Principle . . 468
Developing Ears That Hear:
Responding to the Spirit and the Word 469

Table of Contents: *Planting Churches among the City's Poor, Volume 1*

Appendix
Twenty-five Years of Urban Church Planting among the Poor: A Report 471

An Abridged Church Planting Bibliography 511

The Urban Ministry Institute: Polishing the Stones That the Builders Reject
***How You Can Equip Leaders for Your Church and Ministry* . 519**

Table of Contents:

Planting Churches among the City's Poor, Volume 2

Prologue 11

Part I
Coaching Urban Church Planters:
Resources for Coaches and Mentors 19

Nurturing Church Plant Movements 21

The Nature of Dynamic Church Planting Movements:
Defining the Elements of Effective Church Planting Movements . . 23

Spawning a Church Planting Movement Structure 24

Creating Coherent Urban Church Planting Movements: Discerning the Elements of Authentic Urban Christian Community 25

Enemies of a Vibrant, Dynamic Church Planting Movement. . . 26

A Model of an Urban Church Association. 27

Clement, Calvin, and the LA Urban Pastor's Association:
Review, Reflections, and Recommendations 28

Urban Church Association: Membership Agreement. 39

Coaching Cycle and Duties. 45

The Pauline Church Planting Cycle. 47

The Communal Context of Authentic Christian Leadership . . . 48

Representing God:
Serving Christ as Emissary of Your Local Congregation 49

Representin': Jesus as God's Chosen Representative 65

Understanding Leadership as Representation:
The Six Stages of Formal Proxy. 66

Spiritual Gifts Specifically Mentioned in the New Testament . . 67

Responsibilities of a Coach (Multiple Team Leader) 69

Table of Contents: *Planting Churches among the City's Poor, Volume 2*

Coaching the Leader and the Team 71

Identifying, Training, and Releasing Team Leaders and Coaches in World Impact 73

Equipping the Church Plant Team Member: Developing Workable Training Strategies. 78

Building the Team for Success: Principles of Effective Team Play . . 79

The Church Plant Team: Forming an Apostolic Band 94

The Power and Struggle of Team 95

Missionary Calling: The Ground of Apostolic Mission 98

The SIAFU Network – Assembling God's Warriors: Toward a Strategy to Win the City. 114

Summary of the Capstone Curriculum. 119

Church Planting Charter and Guidance 127

Models of Partnering: Range of Partnership Responses . . . 129

Selecting a Credible Criteria for Independence: Navigating Toward a Healthy Transition 130

Designating Those Who Provide Leadership to Our Church Plant Teams 134

Example of Church Plant Charter: Vickery Meadows 135

Example of Church Plant Charter: Newark Hispanic 136

Church Plant Charter Sample Form 137

Investment, Empowerment, and Assessment: How Leadership as Representation Provides Freedom to Innovate 138

Empowerment: Both Independence and Interdependence . . 139

Our Declaration of Dependence: Freedom in Christ 140

Why Is It Both Prudent and Necessary to Develop a Team Charter? 142

How Do We Authorize Our Church Plant Teams to Operate with Autonomy and Authority? 143

Frequently Asked Questions: Exploring the Ramifications . . 144

Team Leader Identification Grid 148

Overview of Exercise Phases for World Impact's Evangel School of Urban Church Planting . . 150

That We May Be One: Elements of an Integrated Church Planting Movement among the Urban Poor 152

Defining Our Convictions, Distinctives, and Applications: Discerning the Elements of Community Identity 162

Table of Contents:
Planting Churches among the City's Poor, Volume 2

Nurturing Authentic Christian Leadership 163

Four Contexts of Urban Christian Leadership Development . . 164

Developing Urban Christian Leaders: A Profile 165

Team Evaluation Form 166

Associations and Urban Church Planting Movements:
The Efficiency and Reproductive Power of Standardization . . 167

Looking Toward the Horizons:
Facilitating an Association of Urban Congregations 172

Team Facilitation:
Providing Ongoing Input to the Team as Team Leader . . . 177

Team Evaluation:
Providing Formal Feedback for the Team as Coach (MTL) . . 179

Part II
Church Planting Toolkit:
Resources for Planters and Coaches 181

Creedal Theology and Spiritual Calling 183

The Nicene Creed 185

The Nicene Creed with Biblical Support 186

The Apostles' Creed 188

World Impact Affirmation of Faith 189

From Deep Ignorance to Credible Witness:
Stages of Dynamic Growth. 191

Counting the Cost and Hearing the Spirit:
Responding to the Call 192

Fit to Represent: Multiplying Disciples of the Kingdom of God . 197

Summary Outline of the Scriptures 198

Managing Projects for Ministry 203

Davis's Project Gauntlet:
The Dirty Dozen Criteria for New Initiatives 205

Principles of Enterprise Project Management. 207

Project Constraints "Cheat Sheet" 209

Project Management Process 211

Process for TUMI Project Selection and Practice 213

Table of Contents: Planting Churches among the City's Poor, Volume 2

TUMI Policy on Project Process 216
Project Worksheet 218
TUMI Project Protocol: Follow the Yellow Brick Road . . . 221
Project Proposal, Form 1 224
PTC Sample: TUMI Graduation, June 2009 226

Movements and the Great Tradition 231

Defining Church Planting Movements. 233
A Nicene Interpretation of Church Planting Movements. . . 250
Shared Spirituality: Living the Christ Life in Community . . . 251
The Efficiency of Dynamic Standardization: Models Supporting an Integrated Vision of Urban Cross-Cultural Church Planting . 252
Sowing Good Seed: First Steps in Recapturing the Great Tradition through Shared Spirituality 253
Of Whose Spirit Are We? A Primer on Why We Seek to Retrieve the Great Tradition for the City Church 262
The Concept of the Locale Church: The Role of the Regional Church 265
Elements of an Urban Church Planting Movement 269
The Threefold Cord of Urban Cross-Cultural Church Planting Movements 270
The Role of Tradition in Urban Church Planting Movements: Sanctifying the Present by Embodying the Past, Preparing for the Future 271
Dry Wood for a Really Hot Fire: Laying the Foundation for Aggressive Urban Church Planting Movements 283

Administration and Church Structure 305

Bank Accounts and Receiving Gifts 307
Sample New Member's Manual: Anyname Fellowship Church . 309
Effective Worship Leading 316
Sample Membership Application: Anyname Fellowship Church . 328
Membership Commissioning Service: Anyname Fellowship Church 332

Table of Contents: *Planting Churches among the City's Poor, Volume 2*

Drafting a Constitution (Bylaws): Key Tool for Nurturing Community 334
Sample Church Constitution 335
Articles of Incorporation Template 347
Sample Articles of Incorporation 348
Church Financial Processes 351
Petty Cash Account Procedures 354
Church Plant Financial Policies 356
The Church and State 358
Sample 501 (C) (3) Determination Letter 363
IRS Form SS-4: Application for Employer Identification Number . 365
World Impact and Partnership Agreements 367
Conciliation Agreement 371
Sample Partnership Agreement: The Nehemiah Team and World Impact 372
Sample Partnership Agreement: East San Diego Assembly of God and World Impact 374
Sample Partnership Agreement: International Church of the Foursquare Gospel and World Impact . 376
Sample Partnership Agreement: World Impact and the Independent Christian Churches in the Wichita Area 378
Sample Partnership Agreement: World Impact/CEEC Oaklawn Partnership Church Plant . . . 384

Appendix
Twenty-five Years of Urban Church Planting among the Poor: A Report 387

An Abridged Church Planting Bibliography 427

The Urban Ministry Institute: Polishing the Stones That the Builders Reject ***How You Can Equip Leaders for Your Church and Ministry*** **. 435**

Prologue
Planting Churches among the City's Poor, Volumes 1 and 2

Prologue: *Planting Churches among the City's Poor, Vols 1 and 2,* pp. 11-17

What Is an Anthology?

An anthology is a group of resources or items, a collection of some sort, usually selected from a larger whole, most often done by various contributors, authors, or creators themed according to a particular period, but usually concerning a single subject. In other words, an anthology brings together a host of various contributions and reflections all hoping to shed light on the nature of a single theme or enterprise.

By this definition, the following work is in fact that kind of collection on the nature of planting churches, specifically leading teams and coaching planters, among people groups and communities which have historically been the product of benign evangelical neglect. In other words, peoples and communities which, because of their race, or poverty, or violence, or cultural distance, have not been our normal targets for evangelical mission. These documents, graphics, and essays are the result of decades of thought and practice done by urban missionaries among America's urban poor. In their totality they offer a historical snapshot into the various thinking, writing, and reflection that emerged within the World Impact Religious Missionary Order, a community dedicated to planting churches in the most dangerous and least targeted urban communities for the past forty years.

Why Plant Churches among the Urban Poor?

More than two years ago, I wrote a short essay about the phrase "urban poor," whether it was still legitimate to use the term, or perhaps, it should be abandoned as a demeaning and outmoded wording for more accurate and less offensive language (cf. *http://worldimpact.org/empowering-the-urban-poor*.) I wrote the following:

> Since our founding more than forty years ago, World Impact has spoken prophetically regarding God's election of the poor, the benign neglect of the evangelical church of America's inner city poor, and the need for evangelism, discipleship, and church planting in unreached urban poor communities. We believe that credible urban mission must demonstrate the Gospel, testifying in both the proclaimed word and concrete action. In light of this, we have emphasized living in the communities we serve, ministering to the needs of the whole person, as well as to the members of the whole urban family. We have sought this witness with a goal to see communities reached and transformed by Christ, believing that those who live in the city and are poor can be empowered to live in the freedom, wholeness,

Prologue: *Planting Churches among the City's Poor, Vols 1 and 2,* pp. 11-17

> and justice of the Kingdom of God fleshed out in local churches and viable urban church planting movements. All our vision, prayer, and efforts are concentrated on a particular social group, the "urban poor," and our commitment to "empower" them through all facets of our work.

As a missions organization that was founded on a burden to provide empowerment and liberation through the Gospel for the poor, we have wholeheartedly and unashamedly embraced the term. As I said in the essay, "While the phrase 'the urban poor' may be misunderstood or misused, we have chosen to employ it with our own stipulated meanings, informed by biblical theology as well as urban sociology. We employ the term to identify those whom God has commissioned us to serve, as well as to represent God's prophetic call to proclaim Good News to the poor, both to the church and to our society at large." Without any doubt or equivocation, we are committed to see the Kingdom come and advance among those who live in the city, and those whose lives are exposed and vulnerable because of a lack of resources, choices, and options because they are poor. Not only has God chosen them to be rich in faith, he has also declared them to be the very heirs of the forever Kingdom of God to come (James 2.5). To plant churches among the urban poor is to touch the very heart of God, to gather those tender sheaves for which he died, those grains that are ripe for harvest (Matt. 9.35-38).

This anthology brings together a selected grouping of some of the significant essays, graphics, course outlines, articles, and explanations utilized by urban missionaries that have resulted in planting healthy churches among the city's poor. They are not necessarily given in a linear order (according to the time in which they were done), but are rather organized and grouped according to the categories of theology and missiology, leading church plant teams, and coaching urban church planters. Anthologies can be unwieldy and not clean collections, and such is the case here. We have gathered from a wide selection of events, venues, research, and reflection to amass this grouping, and we are confident that the overlap in theme will not deter from the importance of the material within this work.

The sheer extent of venues and publishings that this work draws from is impressive. The list is broad and diverse. For instance, we have drawn materials for this collection from our booklet for cross-cultural church plant teams called *Leading and Feeding Church Planting Teams*, and from our conference for team leaders called *The Timothy Conference*. This

Prologue: *Planting Churches among the City's Poor, Vols 1 and 2,* pp. 11-17

compilation includes materials referenced in World Impact Regional and National leadership meetings, our *Winning the World* TUMI course on church plant movements around the world, and presentations from our *School of Urban Cross-Cultural Church Planting*. We have taken a smattering of graphics from our seminary-level modular series, *The Capstone Curriculum*, and from our World Impact missionary *Candidate Assessment Program*, as well as from actual church plants we have done in the past. We have drawn from many venues, and though full of useful resources, it is not exhaustive! It does represent, however, some of our best thinking from various courses, consultations and reflections on the nature of planting churches among the poor.

We have organized the references in *Planting Churches among the City's Poor* in two complimentary volumes: *Volume One, Theological and Missiological Perspectives for Church Planters*, and *Volume Two, Resources and Tools for Coaches and Teams*. Volume One contains a range of materials related to the whys and wherefores of a biblical theology of mission and church planting, especially how that theology touches upon urban missions, church planting, and the development of healthy congregations and movements.

Volume One, Part I: Developing Urban Congregations, is a reprint of our formative, seminal essay on urban church planting which served as the foundational biblical and theological piece which informed our initial forays into church planting among the poor in the city. *Volume One, Part II: Theological and Missiological Principles and Insights* provides a treasure of resources related to urban missions, ministry among the poor and oppressed, and church planting, including biblical theologies of the Church, retrieval of the Great Tradition among churches which serve the poor, and the role of color, class, and race in making disciples in underserved communities. The resources in *Volume One, Part III, Planting Urban Churches*, concern mainly the theory and practice of actually planting churches among the urban poor, with a focus on the calling, character, and competencies of the church planter, that God-called, Spirit-filled individual who has been led to plant outposts of the Kingdom for Christ among the city's poorest and most vulnerable populations.

Volume Two, Resources and Tools for Coaches and Teams, provides a toolkit, an asset depot containing various materials, tools, and helps to outfit the church plant coach or mentor to lead teams. Additionally, this volume contains numerous specific aids that the planter and his/her team will find invaluable as they engage in their church planting effort.

Prologue: *Planting Churches among the City's Poor, Vols 1 and 2,* pp. 11-17

Volume Two, Part I: Coaching Urban Church Planters, addresses the specific nature of coaching and mentoring church plant leaders and their teams, and seeks to give a broad, compelling outline of the kinds of issues, concerns, and commitments necessary for mentors to understand and do as they coach teams that plant effective churches. And *Volume Two, Part II: The Church Planting Toolkit*, provides a potpourri of miscellaneous articles, graphs, documents, and information relevant to planting a church, including information about financial, state relations, leadership development, forming associations, and equipping for reproduction in church planting movements. In this section you will find abundant particular resources all meant to be helpful for planters, coaches, and associations who desire to plant healthy churches among the poor, both cross-culturally and intra-culturally. These many helps will readily inform your thinking about the nature of planting the individual congregation, forming the structures of a healthy church planting movement, empowering leadership for reproduction, and advancing the Kingdom among the poor in the city.

A Loosely Categorized Collection

In order to aid you in your search for articles and materials that can prove helpful to your inquiries, we have grouped the various items under categories for easier reference. However, because the graphics themselves relate to a host of questions and contexts, you may find that many of the materials can speak to a number of themes, and not merely the category under which they were originally placed.

While the categories are helpful, they ought not to be viewed as authoritative or final. For instance, many of the graphics will undoubtedly speak to a number of different concepts, overlapping between the fields of church planting and coaching church planters, and/or relevant to the design and argument of viable models and theologies that can help us engage the complexity and promise of our unreached urban neighborhoods.

So, when you are perusing this volume, remember to use the table of contents first as a good guide to provide direction to a particular grouping of resources, but also remember that the materials are grouped in a more-or-less generic fashion, and that the materials will have multiple applications, covering a wide range of issues and topics. Do not hesitate to explore different graphics and articles, reading them in new and different contexts than the one we suggest. As a good solid rule, check the table of contents first, but, as you actually look at the resource, think in terms of what other contexts this item might refer to and provide insight into the concepts you explore.

Prologue: *Planting Churches among the City's Poor, Vols 1 and 2,* pp. 11-17

"What Is the Reference for This?"
One of the problems of an anthology of materials within a set community is that, if you do not know the special terms, acronyms, and references which the community is acquainted with, you can lose the original meaning. To comprehend the meaning, you need to know the referent, the initial object or thing to which the reference looks back to. Unfortunately, with more than thirty years having passed, many of the individual articles and the original referents no longer exist; page numbers may be superfluous, reference to articles and essays may be irrelevant, and specific mentionings of previous materials no longer have any foundation. While we have sought to make this perusal of material easier to digest by citing the original referents we could find, alas, there will be citations within many of the documents where the original is lost, misplaced, renamed, or subsumed into another document. Forgive us when you encounter this phenomenon; our desire is to help you access these materials, include the referents where we could, and hope that the original documents are clear enough to navigate through the materials.

One notable exception on the original referent has to do with the letters *CPM* which means "church planting movement(s)." Also, the citations about *C1*, *C2*, and *C3* refer to our thinking about the sub-strata of cultures that interact in the overall American context. (You can understand the original source for this thinking and discussion in a document entitled *Interaction of Class, Culture, and Race.*) The numerous references to the *C1* and related cultures go back to our forty-year use of this thinking grid to comprehend and discuss the implications of culture in urban missions. Please refer to this diagram for our most direct communication on these cultural interactions.

Another issue you should be aware of as you go through this Anthology relates to the use of **designations and terms**. Since *Planting Churches among the City's Poor* is essentially an anthology, we sought to preserve our earlier documents in their original form, and did not go back through the documents and revise the language used in our earliest schools. This is not a major difficulty, however, because although we use different terms than our earlier schools, we have maintained the same functions for the positions. Two terms need to be defined:

- In previous materials, the term used for the church planting supervisor or mentor to whom the team leader reported or received input from was called a ***Multiple Team Leader*** or ***MTL***. Now, in this volume and in our schools, we refer to this role as ***Coach***. All references to ***MTL*** or ***Multiple Team Leader*** in this

Prologue: *Planting Churches among the City's Poor, Vols 1 and 2,* pp. 11-17

volume or in *Planting Churches among the City's Poor* should be understand now as ***Coach***.

- Also, in past schools we used the term ***Team Leader*** for the person in charge of the church plant team and church plant effort. Now, we refer to the person fulfilling this role as the ***Church Planter***.

In terms of language, then, please remember that when you engage materials in the *Anthology* that cite *MTL* or *Multiple Team Leader*, they now ought to be understood as an equivalent terms to Coach, and, the designation *Team Leader* is equivalent now to the designation *Church Planter*.

How to Use This Book

Since the contents of *Planting Churches among the City's Poor* is essentially a collected group of resources on church planting, it lends itself to creative and varied uses. You could simply follow the graphics according to the categories listed, and reflect on the particular graphics and outlines in the order in which they have been organized. You can select particular items and reflect and re-think the subjects based on your own questions and research. Or, you may choose to add to this collection – rearranging, remixing, and re-conceiving the various theologies, approaches, missiological models, and practical protocols we list here, and change and amend them for your context and ministry. This work accumulates a group of materials meant to be processed, rethought, and applied.

Therefore, this work is a varied assortment, an assembly of our dialogues and practices that have informed the ways in which we have conducted ministry that resulted in leaders from the neighborhood who live to serve the neighborhood. Be free in your engagement and application of these materials. Go in any order. Realize, too, that the groupings under the categories are somewhat arbitrary. Frankly, all of the materials included relate in one way or the other to all of the categories given. Use them to help sharpen your own thinking, and provide you with suggestions and insights that can make your own church planting in underserved neighborhoods more biblical and in sync with God's purposes for the church.

In one sense, this collection is a sampler of our theological and ministry tools available for workers on our ministry websites (*www.tumi.org* and *www.worldimpact.org*). These works represent only a fraction of the tens of thousands of pages of curricula, graphics, and course material produced by World Impact missionaries and Institute scholars these

Prologue: *Planting Churches among the City's Poor, Vols 1 and 2,* pp. 11-17

last twenty years. We have learned much about what it means to display the light of the Kingdom in at-risk communities, and we thank God for his leading and direction. Still, we are ever-learning, ever-reforming, ever-willing to learn new things, to explore new directions, and be equipped to do greater things in the name of Christ, for the sake of the city and the poor. Our humble intent is to share the lessons we've learned, not to give the definitive thinking on these matters, but reveal the lessons we have gleaned through planting communities of the Kingdom in the city.

Your interest in this work reveals your connection to three great themes which inform a truly biblical theology of missions: the city, the poor, and the church. Until the Great King returns and makes righteousness roll down like a mighty stream among the nations of the world, we have a sacred obligation to finish the Great Commission (Matt. 28.18-20). While human life began in a garden, it will consummate in a city of God's own building, inhabited by those who were poor in spirit, and will therefore see God. Those from every kindred, tongue, people, and nation who make up the redeemed of God, his church, will live in a new heavens and earth where Christ is Lord. Until that day, we are charged with the task of prophesying deliverance in the name of the Lord to the nations of the earth, whose majority population live in urban communities. The kingdoms of this world will become the Kingdom of our Lord and of his Christ, and he will reign forever (Rev. 11.15).

Your research and engagement in this great mission can contribute to this grand biblical vision. Our prayer is that God will use this work to provide you with greater insight, illumination, and understanding as to how we can plant these outposts of kingdom life among the poorest of the poor in the cities of the world. This is our vision, and our desire is to see the church in America rediscover the fruitfulness and fire of planting churches of among the city's poor. As John Yoder has referred to them, the poor are the "grains of the universe," ripe for harvest. May God send forth qualified spiritual laborers worthy of the risen Christ to plant communities of the Kingdom in his urban harvest.

Rev. Dr. Don L. Davis
March 20, 2015

Table of Contents:
The Evangel Dean Handbook

Welcome Letter **9**

Introduction, Instructions, and Dean School Schedule . . **11**

The Vision and Objectives of the Evangel Dean Training. . . . 11

World Impact, TUMI, and Evangel (History and Relation) . . . 11

Special Instructions 12

Overview Schedule for Dean Training 13

Content Overview 13

Session Core Objectives. 15

Session 1: Evangel's Vision and Strategy

Objectives 19

Devotional 1: Prayer Is the Walkie-Talkie of Faith 21

Team Prayer 1: Let God Arise! Prayer Concert 22

Devotional 2: Freedom in Christ 23

Seminar 1: The Evangel Church Plant School and TUMI's Vision . . 24

Seminar 2: The Evangel Strategy 34

Dean Exercise 1: Seeing the Big Picture: Establishing Context . . 45

Session 2: Evangel and Assessment

Objectives 47

Seminar 3: Assessment and Church Planters
for/from the Urban Poor 49

Seminar 4: Assessing Urban Christian Leaders 61

Seminar 5: Evangel Emphasizes Team 77

Dean Exercise 2: Evaluating Team Effectiveness 101

Team Prayer 2 105

Dean Exercise 3: How Will Evangel Recruit and Assess
Church Planters *for* and *from* the Poor? 106

Team Presentation 1 108

Table of Contents: *The Evangel Dean Handbook*

Session 3: Evangel in Practice

Objectives 109
Seminar 6: What Is a Church? 111
Seminar 7: Church Planting Overview 112
Dean Exercise 4: Seeing the Big Picture: Establishing Values and Vision 113
Devotional 3: The Power of Praise 115
Seminar 8: Using Wisdom in Ministry: The PWR Process . . . 116
Dean Exercise 5: "Prepare" 117
Team Prayer 3 119
Team Presentation 2 120
Seminar 9: Evangel's Launch, Assemble, Nurture, and Transition Sessions 121
Seminar 10: The Importance of Review for Urban Church Planters 138
Dean Exercise 6: Bringing It All Together 139

Session 4: After Evangel

Objectives 143
Seminar 11: The Coach and the Church Plant Team at Evangel . 145
Seminar 12: Charters, Coaches, and the Ongoing PWR Process . 153
Dean Exercise 7: How Will We Coach At and After Evangel? . 156
Seminar 13: Church Plants and Urban Church Associations: The Need for a Local Embrace 158
Seminar 14: Families of Churches: Movements, Associations, and Denominations 176
Dean Exercise 8: How Will Evangel Help New Church Plants Embrace the Church and the World? 179

Session 5: Conclusion

Objectives 181
Devotional 4: God Is a Warrior 183
Team Prayer 4 184
Commissioning Celebration 185

Table of Contents: *The Evangel Dean Handbook*

Appendix

The Nicene Creed with Biblical Support 189

World Impact Affirmation of Faith 191

Our Distinctive: Advancing the Kingdom among the Urban Poor . 193

Overview of TUMI's Resources on the Urban Poor 201

The History of The Urban Ministry Institute 209

Overview of The Urban Ministry Institute's Structure and Strategy 211

Why Develop Extension Centers for Theological Education? . 213

What Is a Satellite of The Urban Ministry Institute? 220

The Strategic Role of the Local Church in Your Institute . . . 222

Three Levels of Ministry Investment 224

Funding Models for Urban Church Plants among the Poor . . 225

Hosting an Evangel School: The Process from A to Z 227

Three Sample Evangel School Budgets 229

World Impact Staff Dean Certification Levels for Evangel . . 233

Evangel Church Plant Charter Form 235

How to Read a Book: Understanding Adler's Four Levels of Reading 236

Urban Church Planting: A Topical Bibliography 237

Top Ten Principles for Elders 257

Preaching and Teaching 262

Suffering for the Gospel: The Cost of Discipleship and Servant-Leadership 264

Streams of Protestant Traditions 266

The Anabaptist Tradition 267

The Anglican Tradition 268

The Baptist Tradition 269

The Dispensational Tradition 271

The Lutheran Tradition 272

The Pentecostal Tradition 273

The Reformed Tradition 274

The Wesleyan Tradition 275

"Framework" for an Urban Church Association 277

Urban Church Association: Membership Form 279

Urban Church Association: Membership Agreement 283

Fortified Urban Church Association: Membership and Associate Guidelines 286

29352511R00110

Made in the USA
San Bernardino, CA
20 January 2016